Love you bye

# SCOTT Mills

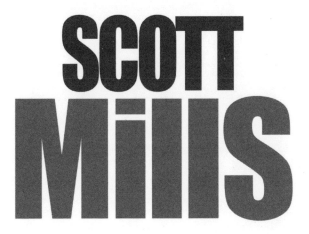

## Love You bye

## MY STORY

sphere

SPHERE

First published in Great Britain in 2012 by Sphere

A CIP catalogue record for this book
is available from the British Library.

ISBN 978-0-7515-4992-8

An Hachette UK Company
www.hachette.co.uk

www.littlebrown.co.uk

To Mum,

for being the best mum and my best friend

Many thanks to Emlyn Dodd for his contribution to the book and his ongoing support in my career. A great colleague and greater friend.

# Contents

# Preface

If you look up 'Scott Mills' on Google – and I hardly ever do this (I think in my whole life I've only done it three or four times ... per day) – the most common searches are:

Is Scott Mills gay?
Is Scott Mills married?
Is Scott Mills dressed as a horse?
Is Scott Mills in *Men In Black 3*?
Is Scott Mills a hermaphrodite?

(*Note*: I might be getting some of those confused with my searches for Lady Gaga.)

You may be reading this book to have those questions answered.

The short answers are:

Yes.
No.
Probably.
I don't know, I haven't seen it.
No, I eat all dairy products.

You may be reading this book because it was given to you as a present by a relative who misheard you when you said 'Chris Moyles'. In which case, the answers to the questions above are:

No.
No.
Probably.
I don't know, I haven't seen it.
No, he eats all dairy products.

You might be reading this book standing in a bookshop, wondering whether or not to buy it. I won't attempt to influence that decision; that's yours to make alone.

All I would say is (buy the book), this is the story of a boy who suffered from crippling shyness and panic attacks, who went on to get his dream job, move in with the star of

*Baywatch*, get a car with his name written down the side, make Katy Perry cry, bleed uncontrollably on live TV, administer a disastrous colonic irrigation, be stalked by an eighties pop star, win awards and somehow avoid the sack for being drunk on air.

In May 2012, as I found myself sitting on a carousel horse in the middle of Baku in Azerbaijan, with Jedward, all I could think to myself was, Where did it all go right?

(Buy the book.)

Scott Mills

London, July 2012

# CHAPTER 1

## Self-diagnosis

Audience figures for radio shows are measured by a company called RAJAR. They give two thousand people a diary to fill in each week, and ask them to tick boxes to show what they've listened to and when. Critics obviously question how accurate this system can be, but this is still how it's done.

I do, however, know precisely how many people tuned in for my first ever radio show; I have the exact figures. It was one. She was my mother. I would have been around eight years old, and my poor mum would sit for hours in my room and listen to me, with my two cassette machines, pretending to be a DJ on Radio 1. Every so often I'd try to double my listening figures with the help of my younger brother, Wesley, but this was very rare and the ratings would soon plummet when he got bored and went out on his bike.

The great outdoors of Southampton just never really appealed to me at that age. Why would you want to be out with friends when you could be doing the chart countdown in your bedroom? I am fully aware how geeky this makes me sound, but that really was me.

Mum – or Sandra from Eastleigh, as she was called when she wanted a shout-out – was my only listener, my biggest encouragement and is to this day my best friend. And it can't have been easy; she's been through a lot over the years. As well as dealing with my neuroses, self-doubt, panic attacks and drinking problem, not to mention the shock of seeing David Hasselhoff naked, she always manages to laugh off the awkward situations I regularly put her in.

When I accidentally locked her in my house with the alarm system on, so when the alarm went off she had to convince the police through the letterbox that she wasn't a burglar, she managed to see the funny side. When I recently took her to a salon to have her eyebrows tinted, she again managed to laugh off the disaster; she has blonde hair but somehow ended up with thick black eyebrows.

You may wonder why Mum has put up with all this. It may be that she feels partly responsible for my existence. She did have quite a key role in my being here, so I think she wants me to turn out all right. The other person with a major say in my being here is my dad Pete. The thing everyone says about my father is that he looks like Bruce Willis; ladies love him. Laura and Beccy, who have worked on my radio show, have both pondered what it would be like to marry my dad, and whether being both my assistant producer and step-mother would make things awkward. This is something too grotesque to even think about, and I will dwell on the idea no more.

I was never really close to my dad growing up, mainly because he worked so hard, and at the time I thought he and I were very different: he's very practical, owned his own removals company, loves football and was quite the lad when he was younger. Nowadays, he and I are much closer and we get on brilliantly, although I still can't see any similarities between us: for a start, he regularly lies about his age – one time he even pretended to be my brother – and then there are his horrendous jokes.

It was Mum who I was closest to, and I will always be grateful to her for regularly getting me out of PE lessons. I was embarrassingly bad at all sports except, bizarrely, the long jump. Thankfully Mum was as good with excuses as I was bad at football, so my PE teacher found that the young Scott Mills was constantly suffering with anything from back pain to bird flu.

Although I didn't hate school and I got on fairly well with people, it was always the escapism of music and my radio shows that made me happy. I think at that age we're all imagining we're somebody else: whether it's pretending we're scoring the winning goal at Wembley in the back garden, singing at the O2 in front of the bedroom mirror, or winning *Ready Steady Cook* while making spaghetti hoops, we're all being someone we're not, and I was no different. I saw being a DJ as a way of acting out a part and it's really only since I've been at Radio 1 that I'm finally comfortable being myself on air.

When I was twelve I decided that just sitting in my room playing at being a DJ wasn't going to get me a job doing it for real. It was also likely to drive my mum insane sooner rather than later. So, for the good of us both, I needed to take the next step.

## FREQUENTLY ASKED QUESTIONS

### #1: *How do I get your job?*

I'm asked this a lot, and it's not 'How did *you* get your job?' or 'How do I get a job like yours?', it's always specifically my job they want for themselves. As if I'm going to tell them that. 'Sure, here's the key, take it!'

However, I can tell you that hospital radio is where I started off. Student radio is also good if you're at university, but I was twelve, so I headed to the hospital.

If you're lucky enough never to have been seriously ill, you may not know what hospital radio is. These are usually registered charities, manned by volunteers, who run radio stations piping entertainment to headphones by patients' bedsides. The volunteers give up their spare time to be DJs, trying to bring some joy to people who often have little to smile about.

Another team of people will give up their evenings and weekends to visit the wards asking if anyone would like to request a song to be played on the station, the answer usually being, 'No, leave me alone.'

Every so often a patient will request their favourite tune, usually 'My Way' by Frank Sinatra or another equally disturbing number to remind them of their possible fate.

When visited again later, the patient will almost certainly not have remembered to listen in for the song they requested.

My hospital radio station was a strange place. I encountered two distinct gangs inside those walls: the Tuesday Night Gang and the Sunday Night Gang. Like the Bloods and the Crips, they loathed each other and never mixed. However, I was scheduled to be a member of both gangs because I was given Tuesdays and Sundays as my evenings to help out.

The Tuesday Night Gang had been in the game for a long time. They were all around sixty years old and veterans of the scene, having played Jim Reeves and Tony Bennett to those wards for as long as anyone could remember. They treated me with suspicion, possibly suspecting I was a Donnie Brasco character, intent on infiltrating their group and undermining them. I watched the Tuesday Night Gang in the studio, studying how they worked and the equipment they used, trying to learn something from every visit. They also watched me like a hawk, determined to discover what I was up to.

The Sunday Night Gang was completely different: they were all about eighteen or nineteen, the young pretenders, the future, willing to let me help out and take part. No wonder the Tuesday Night Gang hated them so much. They would also let me do things I wasn't supposed to, like use the mixing desk, and I absolutely loved it.

The first person who ever sat me in a chair and said, 'Right, go on then, try to do a bit of proper radio,' was Lee Moulsdale, who remains a good friend of mine to this day. It was my chance to show how much I'd learned during my time at the hospital radio station. I recorded a show, operating the equipment and working everything myself. This was my first show outside my bedroom and, although my listening figures hadn't gone up (Lee was the only one), it felt like the first big step towards my future.

I carried on as a member of the Sunday Night Gang and was still treated with suspicion by the Tuesday Nighters for about two years. But then it all went wrong. There was a mole. Someone had blabbed to Tuesday Night that Sunday Night had let me on the radio. That was it; they knew I was trouble. Someone of my age on the radio?

The next thing I knew, I received a letter from the hospital committee saying that I wasn't allowed onto the premises any more – something to do with insurance. Tuesday Night had me 'whacked'; well, my hospital radio career had been 'whacked', and I was told if I ever went inside the building again I would be classed as a trespasser.

I was fourteen years old and had been fired from my dream job. Or, at least, from the job I had hoped would pave the way to my dream. And I wasn't actually being paid, so it may not technically have been a job. But still, I'd been fired.

## THINGS I HAVE LEARNED

### #1: *Plan for a quick getaway*

You may be surprised to learn that hospital radio was the first and last radio station to give me the sack. There are so many stories of DJs being escorted off the premises by security for saying the wrong thing, or having a bad set of RAJAR results, it seems strange that's not happened to me. Yet.

Being fired as a DJ can be quick and it can be brutal. One programme director famously held a presenter meeting where he played them all their new jingles. When one DJ piped up and said, 'My name wasn't on there,' the programme director replied, 'I know. See me in my office after the meeting.'

I've never kept many personal items at work for that very reason. If I'm escorted off the premises I want to make it quick; I'll shove my mug and my signed photo of George Alagiah in a cardboard box and be out the door.

My way back from my hospital radio sacking came through work experience at Ocean FM, a proper radio station. Every Saturday I would turn up and do whatever menial tasks were asked of me. I would happily have dropped out of school and spent all of my time at the studios if I could. Ocean FM gave me a sense of purpose and made me feel much happier and more secure, so it's a mystery as to why I began to suffer from crippling panic attacks at around the same time as I started working there.

## Self-diagnosis

Anxiety runs in my family, and my nan and granddad both suffered very badly. The first time I had an attack it was absolutely terrifying: I had no idea what was happening and I had no control over my body. It came on suddenly and I became obsessed with the idea that I was going to die. Imagine being short of breath and your body feeling as if it has totally seized up. I would get in such a state, and it was my poor mum who had to try to calm me down.

At first the attacks were few and far between, so I could deal with them and I learned to recognise the signs of one coming on. But as time passed they became more frequent and intense; things eventually got so bad I couldn't even leave the house. Mum would regularly have to call the doctor out to me because I was convinced I was going to die during an episode. I used to work myself into such a state that I couldn't see how I would ever feel normal again, and sometimes the only thing that would calm me down in the midst of an attack was knowing that the doctor would arrive to reassure me. Anyone who has experienced anxiety attacks will know exactly what I mean.

I used to sit on the sofa for hours with my head in my hands, crying and saying, 'I can't go out, I can't go out. I can't see anyone, don't leave me,' to my mum over and over again. I would constantly check my pulse, and my heart would race so fast that I would panic more and think I was having a heart attack. Even talking about it now brings all of those horrible feelings back.

Mum would drive me to school and we'd sit outside for ages while I built up the courage to go in. She'd try to tell me everything would be okay, but I couldn't even get out of the car, let alone walk through the gates. It was the same with Ocean FM. I was desperate to go there because I loved it so much, but I'd get short of breath and so stressed I couldn't face leaving the house.

It was like a form of agoraphobia and some days were better than others, but I didn't feel like I could handle anything. I couldn't cope with having to interact with people. Anyone who has ever suffered with any kind of depression or anxiety will understand that feeling of being totally cut off. I hated the thought of being around people, and yet at the same time I desperately wanted to be normal.

Eventually I had to take almost six months off school, and in that time I became a virtual recluse. I didn't want to see anyone. One friend, Laurence, would come round and call for me all the time but I didn't want to go out. It's weird because we'd always been really close – I had even let him be a co-host on some of my pretend radio shows when I was younger – but I just wanted to be on my own or with my mum.

# THINGS I HAVE LEARNED

## #2: *Self-diagnosis is not good for you*

The other problem I had when I was in my mid-teens was always thinking I was ill. That happens with a lot of people who are anxious – they're always thinking their symptoms are a sign of something much more serious. I was convinced I had something really wrong with me and I didn't help myself when I borrowed a self-diagnosis book from the library. Kids don't know how easy they've got it these days: in these modern times the internet can, at the touch of a button, convince you that you have a life-threatening disease. Back then we really had to go out of our way to fuel our paranoia.

**Diseases I was convinced I had, aged fourteen:**

*Fatal familial insomnia*
> Progressively worsening insomnia, leading to
> hallucinations and delirium. No known cure. Death
> within eighteen months.

*Eosinophilia–myalgia syndrome*
> Flu-like neurological condition. No known cure.
> Sometimes fatal.

*Necrotising fasciitis*

> Flesh-eating disease. Treated with high doses of intravenous antibiotics. Without treatment leads to death.

*Gynaecomastia*

> The abnormal development of large mammary glands in males.

*See also*: Monkeypox, Creutzfeldt–Jakob disease, Alien Hand Syndrome, The Plague.

My brother Wesley is four years younger than me, and because we're very different we weren't close growing up. We were usually bickering about something and annoying each other. He once broke one of my *Now That's What I Call Music!* records and I was so furious that it erupted into a full-on fight. What he had done was probably the worst thing you could do to me at that age.

I was fairly well behaved but fragile, but my mum was convinced Wesley would end up a juvenile delinquent. Luckily that prediction turned out to be inaccurate, much to the relief of his fiancée Mandy and my niece Emily.

As we grew up things changed and we only really bonded about five years ago. Wesley is a timber framer and I'd bought a house in Kentish Town. As he's a perfectionist he spent about six months doing the place up. He virtually had to rebuild the top floor and he did an incredible job. I'd go round every night and we'd talk for hours. Things shifted between us: we realised that we had a lot in common and that, actually, we really liked each other. We became extremely close.

My anxiety and panic attacks meant I left school with minimal GCSEs. I wasn't at school for enough time to study for them, and home schooling was out of the question because even that used to stress me out too much. I think I turned up to two exams. I am too ashamed even to look at the certificate to see what I got.

At the time I was gutted that I failed all my exams and it made me feel quite worthless. It really worried my parents too, because I had nothing to fall back on if my grand DJ career plan failed. And as I couldn't even bring myself to walk through the door of the radio station for months, that was looking more and more likely.

After about eight months, with help from my mum, my doctor and some anti-anxiety medication, things finally began to improve. Mum and I agreed that the next step was for me to go back to Ocean FM. Somehow I knew that if I could just make it through the door I would be okay.

I remember Mum driving me to the station on my first day

back so clearly. I felt a mixture of panic and excitement, and I was doing deep breathing throughout the entire journey. We sat in the car park for a good half an hour while she calmed me down and did her best to convince me that everything would be okay. Then I got out of the car, walked towards the main radio station entrance, pushed open the door and walked in.

Rather than feeling stressed about being back there, it actually made me feel calm. I don't know if it was because it was a place I knew and felt comfortable in, but I felt happy for the first time in ages. It was a massive accomplishment for me to have actually left home, and the outside world wasn't anywhere near as scary as I'd built it up to be.

Over time, being back at the radio station really helped to build up my confidence. Although it took me a while, I was able to get my anxiety down to a manageable level and lead a normal life again.

## THINGS I HAVE LEARNED

### #3: *People really do say 'I'll make you a star!'*

I always thought that only happened in movies. Remember the film *Cocktail*? Doug says, 'When you see the colour of their panties, you know you've got talent. Stick with me, son, and I'll make you a star.'

I never thought anyone would say that to me, especially not the boss of Ocean FM in Hampshire, but he did. Though, for legal reasons, I should point out there was no mention of panties.

Chris Carnegy was the programme director, and stopped me as I was walking down the corridor. He'd seen me around the studios and vice versa, but I'd always been too scared to talk to him. After a brief chat he asked if I wanted to be on the radio one day, and I replied nervously, 'Yes, I'd really love to.'

Summer was coming up, and he explained that was when they often needed cover for people who were away on holiday. Although he couldn't promise anything, he said that he would see if he could get me some shifts. I can't even remember what, or even if, I replied, because I was so stunned.

And then it happened, just like in the movies. As he walked away he said with a smile over his shoulder, 'Send me a tape and I'll make you a star.'

I remember thinking it was the coolest thing I ever heard. People should say that more, I think. It brought a certain glamour to a small local radio station.


Back then I used to spend hours sitting up into the early hours either at home or at the studio making demo tapes of radio shows. My audience figures had plummeted over the last few years: I had gone from one listener to zero. But Chris's offer to listen to my demo was a chance to get some real-life listeners who weren't related to me.

I recorded a new demo and handed it to Chris. Amazingly, after taking it away and listening to it, he took a chance and put me on air.

I was only given a one-off show, filling in for a presenter who was away, but it was a massive deal. It was my first paid radio work and all I could do was hope for the best. I still remember it so clearly. The news finished and I nervously read out the weather. I played a jingle, then a song.

I was still suffering with pretty bad anxiety at times. My mum dropped me off before I was due to start the show and I started saying I couldn't do it. She eventually managed to talk me round by telling me that it could be the beginning of something I could do for the rest of my life.

My slot was a late-night on a Sunday and it certainly wasn't perfect. But I got through it and Chris called me afterwards to congratulate me.

He was honest and said that a lot of things needed improving, but he also said that he could see past my nerves so he was willing to give me another opportunity to show what I could do.

Everybody has someone about whom they can say, 'Without them, none of this would have happened.' For me that person was Chris Carnegy. There was no reason for him to give me a chance:

1. I was a nervous wreck.
2. I would need to get permission from my parents whenever he offered me a shift.
3. I wasn't even that good.

But Chris heard something he liked and for the rest of that summer, whenever presenters went on holiday he got me to fill in for them. The more shows I did the more comfortable I got. Sometimes I'd be on air four or five times a week and I began to relax into it and sound much more natural.

Ocean FM was part of a larger broadcasting company with several different radio stations in the same building, so I'd jump between them when I was needed. I'd be playing chart hits on Power FM, then two hours later I'd be playing sixties music on Gold AM.

I was sixteen when all of this was going on. The summer of 1989 is a time I'll never forget because it all felt a bit magical. It still does.

## CHAPTER 2

# A Car with My Name on It

I carried on working at Ocean FM whenever they needed me, and later that year the unimaginable happened: I signed my first proper contract. I had been offered my own show. Five days a week! From one until six! In the *morning*?

The hours were hardly sociable, so I decided I needed some transport.

A few weeks later I collected my mean machine and rode it home. Dr Fox may have had a Harley-Davidson, but I was the proud owner of a Honda Vision scooter.

I felt true freedom, finishing my show at six in the morning, getting on my scooter and riding full pelt at thirty miles an hour back home. By the time I got there, about forty minutes later, I would be so cold Mum would have to sit me next to the radiator to thaw me out.

It soon became clear that this was not a vehicle to be seen on in public; I was so embarrassed by my scooter that I used to park it around the corner from the radio station so no one could see it.

# FREQUENTLY ASKED QUESTIONS

## #2: *When did you first realise you were gay?*

A lot of people seem to think there's a moment when a big light goes on and it's 'PING! Oh my God, I'm gayyy!' That certainly wasn't the case with me.

There was a point when I realised that maybe girls weren't for me, though. I was about fifteen. One of my friends had a car, and I remember one day we went down to Weston seafront in Southampton with two girls, his girlfriend at the time and her friend Sammi. She was the kind of Sammi who would have put a smiley face on top of the 'i' in her name. It was quite clear that Sammi fancied me, and before I knew it she was trying to snog my face off in the back of my mate's Vauxhall.

I almost had to prise her off, and I went home that night feeling annoyed that I didn't like her in the way she liked me.

She called my home phone the next day and told me that maybe we should just be friends. I agreed. I never saw her again.

I met my first ever boyfriend, whom I'll call Nathan, at around this time. He was a couple of years older than me with his own place, and I was so into him, in the way you are when you're that age. We were friends first, but we started spending more and more time together and I fell in love for the first time.

But what would my parents say? I had kept the whole thing a secret, fearing their reaction, but after a few months I decided I had to do the right thing and tell my family I was gay.

I was scared about what they'd say, but finally I plucked up the courage and sat down to talk with Mum. I broke down in tears almost immediately and simply told her, 'Mum, I'm gay.'

'I know,' she replied.

I wasn't expecting that.

I was probably fearing my brother's reaction the most, and Mum said she would break the news to him gently.

'Wesley, Scott's gay,' she said.

'I know.'

It took Dad a little while to get his head around it – he was a bit funny for a while. Even though he had had his suspicions, as everybody obviously did, I think it was hard for him. After he'd had some time to get used to the idea he was really supportive, but I think it was a lot for him to come to terms with. I don't think either of my parents had met anyone gay before, or not knowingly, anyway.

After about a year I moved in with Nathan. I had left home and my parents, and Littlehampton was my oyster. There was a casino, the Look & Sea Visitor Centre and, of course, the town is home to the famous Harbour Park amusement park, 'Where the FUN will never set!'

I visited none of these places; the hours I was working and the fact that I was the most super-square person you could ever meet, meant that Nathan and I would go to work, then go home and eat, sleep, wake up and do it all again. We didn't even drink. I was living the life of a forty-five-year-old when I was seventeen, and I was quite happy with that at the time.

The journey to work was too far for my scooter. Instead, I'd leave at nine o'clock each night and get a train to Swanwick for about eleven, then walk to the radio station in Park Gate. I'd be on air from one to six, then travel back to Littlehampton and repeat, repeat, repeat.

Sometimes Nathan drove, if he was on a night shift. We would go in together and I would sleep in his car outside the radio station for a few hours, until I had to go on air. It was a tiny car and so cold and uncomfortable that I don't think I ever slept properly. I was exhausted most of the time.

Just before Christmas 1990 a new boss joined the Ocean Group. His name was Jeremy Scott and one of his first ideas was to tell all the DJs he'd decided to have a clear-out so many of them wouldn't have a job in January. Understandably, that festive season wasn't the most cheerful.

By this time I had moved to the Drivetime show on Power FM. It played current music – a bit like Radio 1 – so it suited me better.

Jeremy used to terrify me. He would ring the studio to let me know that he was listening in his car, and that I'd 'better be good'. Those calls would frighten the life out of me.

I had an incredibly tense Christmas, most of which was spent trying to think of other things I could possibly do with my life. In January, Jeremy called the staff into his office one by one. I remember going in, thinking, This is it, it's all over. But I was one of the lucky ones. Jeremy spared me.

Despite being very relieved, I knew things were unstable at the station and I started to feel unhappy about working there. Everyone felt they could be sacked at any moment, and when morale is bad at a radio station I really think the listeners can tell. The bad atmosphere was having a serious knock-on effect on everyone working at Ocean.

My mum noticed that I was quite down about things and she even said to me one day, 'I do think you're good at the radio, but I'm not sure you're cut out for it. It seems like it's quite a tough business and I don't think it's for you. It seems pretty cut-throat and I don't want you to end up getting hurt.'

In a way she was right because I was still a nervous little teenager and I did let things get to me. But now I had my foot in the door I wasn't about to turn and run. Ocean wasn't going to drive me out through fear. I would stand my ground. I had made up my mind: this was my dream and I was not going to be denied. A few weeks later I left.


A man named Steve had called the newsroom at Ocean and left a message for me. I had never heard of him, but called him back. He explained that he was Steve Orchard, the programme controller at GWR in Bristol, and asked if I would be interested in a move.

The Ocean Group was, on the whole, an incredible experience. It was a big factor in helping me to become more outgoing and it was thanks to Ocean that I really found my feet as a presenter. Because of that I felt really guilty about leaving, and on the day I told them I was going they made me feel like I had let them down.

I had worked my way up from being a tea boy to having a full-time DJ job, but now I was leaving for something bigger and better. Anyone in my position would have done the same.

Jeremy reacted exactly as I expected him to. He was angry and told me I was making a huge mistake. When that didn't work, he changed tack. He took me out for dinner and said he really didn't want me to go. It was like a bizarre relationship break-up. I was hoping he wouldn't make a scene and be holding onto my leg as I left the restaurant. Given that I had spent the past twelve months or so feeling like Jeremy was going to sack me at any time, I didn't feel an enormous amount of loyalty towards him and I can't deny that part of me enjoyed telling him I was leaving. For once, he wasn't in control. It felt good. Despite the sign at Harbour Park, the fun had set on Littlehampton and I left the south coast.

Bristol was a total revelation. I had managed to wangle an extra £2500 on my salary, so I was on £18,500 in my new job, which seemed like an absolute fortune. Also, my new show was from ten in the morning until one, so after two years of working at night I could go out and drink and make new friends ... and meet boys. Sadly, Nathan and I split up when I moved to Bristol. I was by now out of my teens but hadn't done anything exciting in my life when it came to going out.

I hadn't hung out with friends. I'd spent my life in a studio working crap hours or stayed in the house. I started discovering new things and having a social life, and that put a strain on our relationship. Plus I was living quite far away and working loads, so we didn't get to see each other very much. Nathan was my first love, and it was amazing, but I had moved to a new place and had a completely new life. For the first time ever I was going out to bars and getting friends of my own age.

I met so many great people in Bristol, like Neil and Roger, who are still two of my best friends. They both work in radio and we see each other all the time. They really looked after me at a time when Bristol felt quite big and scary.

## THINGS I HAVE LEARNED

### #4: All the best people fail their driving test on the first attempt

That's what my friends told me when I came back from the test centre feeling dejected. It's always good to hear a cliché when something bad has happened. You've been dumped – 'Plenty more fish in the sea'. Your landlord says your rent is late and he may have to litigate – 'Don't worry, be happy'.

But there is apparently some truth to this one. A lot of the best drivers did fail first time. Even Jenson Button didn't pass his first driving test.

He did at least pass his second one. I didn't. I also failed my third test.

You don't often hear 'all the best people pass *fourth* time'.

Mariah Carey passed on her fourth attempt and I certainly wouldn't get in a car that she was driving.

I still blame freak occurrences for my failures. During one test I was halfway through doing a three-point turn when I saw a cat run underneath the car. I stopped and waited for it to come out the other side. But it didn't. It had decided to stay underneath the car. I was at a standstill in the middle of the road and a cat had decided to have a nap under my car, in the middle of my driving test. As traffic on both sides of the road had stopped, with me blocking the whole street, I looked at the examiner. What do you do in that situation? The blaring car horns didn't help me think straight either. I didn't want to run over the cat, so we just sat there for what felt like three weeks. I'm still not sure what the right thing to do would have been. What would Mariah Carey have done? She almost certainly wouldn't have bought a Nissan Bluebird when she finally passed her test, but that's just one of the things that sets Carey and myself apart.

I met my second proper boyfriend while I was working at GWR – let's call him James. Once again, we were just mates to start with, then more. Well, I say proper boyfriend. We were really in love, inseparable in fact. He made me so happy. But with James there were two problems. First, he was straight, and second, he was very religious. He wasn't sure the idea of loving me was going down well with God. I tried to reason with him but, as usual, the omnipotent deity won over the local-radio DJ.

That was my first real heartbreak. I saw him regularly and our relationship was on and off for well over a year. I knew I was fighting a losing battle, but I always hoped I could convince him.

One time, I was so desperate to see him again that I invited him on a picnic. I made up a massive hamper full of food and drink, but when I phoned him he said he didn't think it was a good idea. I stood in the phone box crying my eyes out and begging him to see me. Then, naturally, every song I played on the radio would remind me of him. GWR wasn't the best radio station to be on when you were going through a break-up; I would be sitting on my own in a room for three hours, playing nothing but love songs. Luckily R.E.M. were on hand, roughly once every hour and a half, to tell me that 'Everybody Hurts'.

James is now married. When he met his wife he told her the whole story and admitted he'd been in love with me. He's a great guy and we're still in touch, but at the time it was a horrible thing to go through. I don't think I've felt quite the same way about anyone since.

As a result of making friends and hanging out in pubs, I became much more outgoing. I had a bit of a life! But I was still quite shy around people I didn't know, so one of my main concerns when I joined GWR was having to do celebrity interviews. The notion of talking to a famous person filled me with fear. Luckily, no famous people ever seemed to come our way, so I felt pretty safe in the GWR building. Until one day, when I arrived in the office and something didn't feel right. *Star Wars* fans would describe it as a 'great disturbance in the Force'. There was someone different in the building; I smelt him before I actually saw him. An aftershave so strong it actually made my eyes water. Then I turned a corner and saw him. He had his back to me, and was dressed all in leather. He was commanding the room, people were flocking around him; I saw him nodding confidently, holding court with a story. I couldn't hear what he was saying but it must have been hilarious because everyone was laughing. As I walked into the room he turned around. It was Dr Fox. In our office. I was starstruck. Here in front of me was the very personification of cool. Our eyes met and I think in that moment we made a connection. Perhaps he sensed he was in the presence of a fellow bike enthusiast. He had a Harley-Davidson, I had a Honda Vision. I wondered if, in his mind, he'd seen his young self walk into that room. His glance at me must have lasted a split-second but it meant something. Then, very professionally, he turned back around and carried on telling his hilarious anecdote. I didn't speak to him that day and didn't see him again until many years later when I spotted him in London's glamorous restaurant, Planet Hollywood. To this day Dr Fox pretends he doesn't remember that moment we shared in the offices of GWR, but it will stay with me for ever.

## THINGS I HAVE LEARNED

### #5: Nothing says 'you've made it' like a car with your name written on the side

At this time there was a man working at GWR who was the go-to guy if you wanted anything. He was very high up in sales and if you talked to him nicely he could wangle you a free car with your name on it. This was the ultimate status symbol: a car with your own name written on each side of the vehicle, sometimes surrounded by musical notes.

If you didn't have one of those in local radio circles you were no one.

I went to see him. His name was Jeremy Kyle. You may have heard of him, thanks to his popular, all-shouting, all-DNA-testing ITV show.

I've always liked Jeremy, he's very smart and good to talk to. That day I was also hugely grateful that he managed to swing it so that I got a Toyota with 'Scott Mills' up the side. Underneath my name were the words 'GWR – no rap less chat' and some musical notes.

This was the big time. I thought there was something magical about having a car like that. I clearly remember the first time I pulled up at a set of traffic lights in that Toyota. I looked around and people were staring. A man eating a burger outside McDonald's stopped mid-chew and stood there, reading the side of my car. The lights changed to green and I turned back to him and smiled. The man with the burger did the international sign for 'wanker' and I sped off.

It soon became clear that, outside local radio circles, a car with your name on the side was the funniest thing people had ever seen. The Toyota was now an embarrassment but, because they had spent money on it, GWR made sure I turned up at every event driving it.

*Some places I took the Scott Mills 'no rap less chat' car to:*

1. The Bristol Toilet Roll Championships
   They had paid for advertising on the network, so I had to wrap myself in loo roll.
2. Free Wash Friday
   My whole show came from the forecourt of Brian Brothers' garage, announcing over the radio that anyone who came along would get a free car-and-screen wash.
3. The GWR Roadshow
   Where once our tent blew away and the *Daily Star* wrote the station a letter, calling it a 'fucking kite'.
4. A milk promotion
   I had to dress up as a cow and go round to people's houses and moo at them.

It wasn't all fun, though. I also had my first and hopefully last near-death experience while I was working at GWR. I used to travel around in a specially adapted outside broadcast van with a guy called Martin. When you opened the roof a massive mast would pop up, enabling you to broadcast from wherever you were. It was all very primitive, but seemed cutting-edge at the time.

Once we were driving down the Bath Road and I suddenly felt the van being pulled back sharply. The front wheels were coming off the ground and we were starting to do a wheelie, in a van! Martin and I grabbed our seats till our knuckles went white, and we both realised what had happened. Martin had left the mast up after we'd finished the broadcast and, as we were driving, it had become tangled up in some phone lines. If they had been electric cables we'd have been killed immediately. Two radio engineers in Gloucester had done exactly that a year earlier and both of them had died, so we had a very lucky escape.

Near-death experiences aside, Bristol is such a great city that if I wasn't living in London I'd move back there tomorrow. I stayed for two years and it was a really special time. The job was fun, my friends were great and I had enough cash to do whatever I wanted to do. I couldn't have been happier.

## THINGS I HAVE LEARNED

### #6: *People really do have secret meetings in motorway service stations*

Just as I thought the 'I'll make you a star' line was only used in films, I was convinced that covert meetings in motorway service stations only happened in spy series. Again, I was wrong.

I pulled into the car park of Frankley Services, on the M5 near Birmingham. I was halfway between Birmingham and Manchester, and was there to meet a complete stranger. I had no idea what the man looked like, but I needn't have worried: a man in a trench coat saw me in my car and started walking towards me. As he got into the passenger seat I wondered how he knew it was me. Then I quickly remembered the words 'Scott Mills – no rap less chat' written on my car.

The man was Mark Story; he worked for Key 103 in Manchester and had phoned me, wanting to talk about a job they had at their radio station.

We went for a coffee in the service station and I expected a tough interview or horrendous grilling from him. But he simply offered me the job. In the dank surroundings of a motorway coffee shop, with the smell of greasy food in the air, I had just been offered the biggest job of my radio career.

At the time, Key 103 was one of the 'Big Five' (the others were

Capital FM in London, BRMB in Birmingham, Clyde in Glasgow and Metro in Newcastle). All DJs worth their salt wanted to work at one of those stations. Radio 1 was massive but untouchable: getting a job there wasn't even thought about – everyone wanted to do it but the chances were so minimal you didn't let yourself consider it could happen. At one point, while I was at GWR, I thought I would send Radio 1 a tape on the off chance. They sent me a letter, telling me that if I kept on contacting them I would end up on the 'DJ pest pile', which is reserved for people who are deemed to be a pain in the arse.

Leaving Bristol proved hard in more ways than one. When I announced to GWR that I was leaving they were incredibly annoyed. They told me I was in breach of contract and did everything they could to stop me going. I ended up sending and receiving solicitors' letters for the next year, trying to get back loads of money they owed me. In the end I won the case, but it was a sour end to what had been a fantastic time.

I didn't have much opportunity to go flat-hunting before I moved to Manchester so I took more or less the first place I found that was habitable, which turned out to be a granny flat in Sale. Once the initial buzz of moving there wore off, I felt completely isolated. Whereas in Bristol I'd made friends and fitted in really quickly, Manchester was the total opposite. I don't think I've ever felt more alone than I did in the first six months I spent there.

It was 1993, Christmas was just around the corner and I was all on my own. My show didn't start until ten at night so I literally had nothing to do until eight, when I'd have to leave for work.

I missed James like mad and was still really hurt by our break-up, which didn't help matters. Although, looking back, moving to Manchester and away from the situation was one of the best things I could have done.

Probably the lowest point for me was when I went to buy a Christmas tree. I got in my new Nissan Bluebird and drove it to Sale New Road, where I picked out the nicest tree I could find. I paid a fortune for it and dragged it into the house, put it up and spent ages decorating it. Then I stood back and looked at it thinking, What's the point? There's no one here. No one will see it apart from me. I'd made one friend through work, Danny, who had promised to pop by that day and see the tree but he hadn't turned up. I was alone with a giant tree, some decorations and an Indian meal for one.

1994 didn't get off to a great start as my mum and dad decided they were officially going to split up. It had been on the cards because they had been apart for a while, but it was still awful when it actually happened. All I wanted was to be there for Mum, but I was so far away and working so much that it was impossible for me to get back to see her very often. She would phone me up sobbing her eyes out and I was totally heartbroken for her. We've always been close – we say that we're each other's best friend – and at that time we could easily spend two or three hours on the phone talking everything through. We got through those horrible times together, and I don't know what we would have done without each other.

Things began to pick up, though. Within six months of starting on the Key 103 evening show the bosses came to me and said that Gary King, who had been hosting the morning show, was leaving to work on the launch of the all-new Virgin Radio in London. When they offered me the chance to take over his show I was overwhelmed. Key 103 was getting the biggest audience figures in the country outside London, so it was a massive deal.

## THINGS I HAVE LEARNED

### #7: *Never turn down a meal with Noddy Holder*

Noddy Holder from Slade was working at Key 103 at this time. I would hear his voice around the building and just think, It's him, it's the man off of Christmas. I'll never forget him coming up to me one day and saying, 'Fair play to you, Scott. You've done all right for yourself.'

I replied, 'Thanks, Noddy, you're the man from Slade.'

He looked at me quizzically but agreed that yes, that was him.

Noddy is such a nice guy; soon after that initially awkward meeting I'd often go out for drinks with him and chat about all things music. Just before Christmas in 1994 he invited me out for a meal. I couldn't get my head round the idea: Christmas dinner with Noddy Holder. Naturally, he suggested a Chinese restaurant and as we sat there chatting another man joined our table. To my surprise it was his friend Roy Wood from Wizzard, who sang 'I Wish It Could Be Christmas Everyday'.

Sitting there that night, laughing my head off, I thought back to the previous Christmas and how unhappy I'd been. It made me realise how much things can change in a year. Twelve months earlier I'd been lonely and sad, but here I was hosting one of the biggest radio shows in the country and eating festive noodles with the two most important people in the Christmas story apart from Jesus and all those other folks. The contrast was unbelievable. Every time anyone entered the restaurant I'd look up, expecting it to be Shakin' Stevens or Jona Lewie or one of their other Christmas mates. One man, who looked a bit like Shane MacGowan, did come in, but he was quickly removed by the manager.

*

I got a new company car when I was in Manchester, and I was mortified to see it once again had my name written on the side. This time it said 'Scott Mills – Key 103 – Salford Quays Toyota'. When I stopped at crossings or traffic lights I would avoid eye contact with passers-by, but I would still hear them. Occasionally I would forget I was driving a car with my name on the side but as soon as I saw the people making 'wanker' signs at me I'd remember.

## THINGS I HAVE LEARNED

### #8: Radio stations are never glamorous

People are always disappointed when they arrive at radio stations. I guess because you have an image in your mind about what the place looks like, it never measures up. In our listeners' minds Key 103 probably wasn't situated in the most disgusting, piss-stinking, disused seventies shopping centre you can imagine, but in reality that's exactly where it was. Key 103 was the only business there, apart from Air Iraq and a fish and chip shop, which meant the studios constantly smelt of grease and hot fat, which seeped up through the floor.

If Joan Collins had been told that she certainly wouldn't have visited the station. Joan was classed as a very special visitor so she was given a very special welcome; security had even arranged for the escalators to be switched on for her. I will never forget the look on her face as, decked out in high heels and fur coat, she tiptoed through the wee-drenched, junkie-filled concrete hall which led to our studios. Her look of disdain will stay with me for ever. She, however, did not stay for long.

## THINGS I HAVE LEARNED

### #9: *When people start throwing bottles, it's time to leave*

This may seem obvious, but for some reason, one evening I didn't take the hint.

I still did a lot of promotional work while I was in Manchester, but thankfully I was no longer expected to dress up as a cow or stand on garage forecourts. It was a lot more dangerous.

There was a long-term promotion for Morgan's Spiced Rum which involved me going to nightclubs every Friday and giving people the chance to win holidays and other prizes. After we'd exhausted all of the central Manchester clubs and bars, Key 103 decided that we should start targeting places in the surrounding areas, like Moss Side. Back then those places were no-go areas. Unless, of course, you were being paid to host a booze promotion.

I was assigned a tour manager who travelled around with me for protection, but I still felt like I should have drunk several bottles of the stuff before I ventured into most of the pubs. I remember going into Oldham and spotting a lot of mounted police by about seven o'clock in the evening, which I don't think is generally a good sign.

One evening I went to Audenshaw, where I was supposed to visit several pubs. When I walked into the first bar everyone put their pints down and turned round to stare at me, a fat, terrified young Southerner.

It went silent, another moment that only usually happens in films. I got up on a makeshift stage with my microphone and greeted my audience. 'Good evening,' I said in a nervous squeak. A glass hurtled past me and smashed on the wall behind. I stopped for a split-second, looked down at my script and carried on. 'Morgan's Spiced—' Smash! A bottle landed at my feet. I really wasn't sure what to do, and luckily the tour manager spotted this. He ran over, literally pulling me off the stage, and said, 'We've got to go.'

I dropped the mic and we were barely at the door before glasses and bottles were being hurled and people were punching each other. Again, it was like a film; I could actually hear glass breaking as we fled.

Later the same night we tried our luck in a pub in Ashton-under-Lyne. This time, I was halfway through my sales pitch about the amazing rum when I saw a guy pick up a glass and shove it into another man's face. Needless to say, we decided to get the hell out of there. As we were hurrying to leave we saw the injured guy get carried out. Then a woman came out from behind the bar, swept up the glass, washed away the blood and put the music back on, and everything went back to normal. I learned very quickly: when the glasses come hurtling towards you, get the hell out.

I had stayed single for quite a long time after James, but towards the end of my time in Manchester I started seeing a guy called Darren. He was one of those guys who I knew was bad news, but of course that was part of the attraction. I really fancied him but at the same time didn't trust him. He was the kind of person I would never go for in a million years now.

I had actually met him a while ago, but one day he turned up in Manchester and announced that he was moving in with me. We had been seeing each other for a bit, and he just arrived in a van with all his stuff. I was confused and didn't know how to turn him away. Nobody had ever moved in unannounced before.

I knew it wasn't a good idea for us to be living together. He was also so aggressive that, at times, I was properly scared.

Thankfully Darren made our break-up quite easy. Six months after he moved in I went on holiday and, in another scene straight from a movie, I arrived back to find him in bed with my friend. Yes, that really can happen in real life.

I remember grabbing him and shouting at him – I even pinned him to the wall with my hand around his throat, which was very out of character for me, but I was so angry. Then I threw him and all of his stuff out of the flat.

Even though I'd always kind of known he was dodgy I was still really hurt by Darren's betrayal. I should never have got involved with him, but it was one of those young things where I thought it would be okay and that I could change him. That never works. I know that now.

Shortly after my break-up with Darren my life completely changed once again. I was working with a great guy called Keith Pringle and he landed a job on the launch of Heart FM in London. He asked if I wanted to join the crew and I jumped at the chance. I knew it would be the most amazing opportunity, and if I wanted to be taken seriously as a DJ I had to keep moving on and up.

London was the big one.

# CHAPTER 3

# In at the Deep End

Heart was a good place to work in lots of ways, but I think that back then, at twenty-two, I was too young to be there.

The people were great, but the place was crawling with 'consultants'. Lots of radio stations hire consultants, usually from the US or Australia, and pay them a fortune to tell everyone how *they* do it back home.

This means the DJs are constantly being told off for not mentioning London in a link, or slightly deviating from the brand message. You can always tell when a consultant has been in: the DJs' links get more and more formulaic, and any personality is quickly sucked from their shows.

I didn't have a bad time at Heart, but I felt like I clocked in and clocked out, and didn't have a lot of freedom to do what

I wanted with my show. It wasn't much of a challenge because you weren't really allowed to say anything and I was broadcasting to an older audience than I'd been used to at Key.

## THINGS I HAVE LEARNED

### #10: *You never truly know somebody until you've lived with them*

My first priority in London was finding somewhere to live, but when I looked at what I could rent for the same money I had been spending in Manchester it was depressing. I had been living in a three-bedroomed house in Worsley, near where Ryan Giggs lived, and the equivalent in London was a tiny studio flat in the middle of nowhere, miles from the Tube.

A girl I knew from Manchester had recently come to London and suggested I move in with her, which seemed like the perfect solution.

I was relieved to be living with someone I knew. I had other friends in London but a lot of them had their own places or lived with partners, and the flat itself was really nice.

I thought we got on well, until I moved in. She was religious, and very early on made it clear that she didn't agree with a lot of things I did – even drinking coffee. I was the lodger but I would be told off as if I were a small child. She disapproved of everything from what I ate to the books I read. She was like the nagging wife from a seventies sitcom.

Then things started to get weird. When she wasn't haranguing me like an old *Coronation Street* character she behaved as though we were a couple. If I wasn't in for the evening she would get really sulky and not talk to me when I came home. This was my landlady!

Then, in the morning, she would demand a hug, and I could feel her getting more and more clingy.

People who were around at the time say she was in love with me, and while I couldn't see it then, I fear that may have been the case.

One evening I'd been out for a few drinks and I brought some friends back to the flat. As I put my key in the door she was standing in front of me looking really upset and saying, 'Where have you been?'

Every so often I would make sure I hadn't given her the wrong idea.

'I'm gay,' I would say.

'I know,' she would reply, sounding like my mother.

The whole situation got much worse when I got a boyfriend. Her mum rang the home phone one day to rant at me: 'What have you been doing to my daughter? She's so upset.'

It got to the stage where I didn't want to go home so would go out with friends and then wait in the street until her bedroom light went out. I'd then let myself in and run to my bedroom. I virtually lived in my room for months so I could avoid her.

Remember, this was my landlady, and someone who up until I'd moved in had been a friend.

It came to a head one weekend. My boyfriend lived in Wales, so he used to come and stay at the weekend. One Saturday afternoon we got home to find her mum, not content with ranting on the phone, had actually turned up.

Her mum was a large woman who did, strangely, look like an overbearing wife from a seventies sitcom.

She started to rant again.

'Do you know how much you've upset my daughter?'

I hate confrontation, so actually started apologising. My boyfriend, however, was having none of it. Before long he was accusing her of being crazy while she was mocking him for being gay.

As the two of them exchanged insults I walked out of the house and never went back.

The Welsh boyfriend, while being feisty, also did that thing of being totally in love one minute and absolutely not bothered the next, so I got dumped. After a while I started dating a cute posh guy called Matt. He was a conductor, and he even took me to the Proms once. I liked Matt, but the relationship didn't really go anywhere and we split up.

About a year after I joined Heart I went to the Sony Radio Awards. Every industry has its major award ceremony and the Sonys is ours. It is known as the Radio Oscars but then, every industry's award ceremony is compared to the Oscars, isn't it? 'Welcome to the Growlers, the Oscars of the artisan pork pie industry!'

Depending on who you ask, there are two definitions of the Sony Radio Awards:

1. An evening honouring the best broadcasters in the UK, presenting them with the ultimate accolade voted for by their peers.
2. A long, boring, drunken evening where the meaningless awards are given out for purely political reasons.

Your own definition simply depends on whether or not you've just won an award.

The thing I quite like about the Sonys is that, once a bit of wine has been consumed, there's very little pretence. There's none of that fake Oscars smiling and pretending you're happy that your rival has just won. Winners are sometimes booed by their competitors as much as they are cheered by their colleagues.

The first time I attended the Sonys with Heart I met a guy called Simon Willis. He worked for Radio 1 and suggested that I send him a demo of the kind of show I'd like to do for the station.

I hadn't seriously thought about trying out for Radio 1, apart from the tape and letter I'd sent them years earlier. I didn't see how it would be any different, but it was still my dream job. This guy had offered me what could be a huge opportunity, so I wasn't about to turn it down.

The only problem was, I couldn't be sure whether Simon would remember asking me to send him a demo. After a few days of calling him, true to his word he said that if I sent something over to him he'd give it a listen and get back to me. I sent the tapes off and hoped for the best, but after getting several polite refusals I conceded defeat. Maybe Radio 1 wasn't for me.

Several months later I decided to try again. Once again I sent off a few demos and this time was invited to do a pilot in the Radio 1 studios.

As I've already mentioned, radio studios are never very

glamorous places, but the first time I arrived at Radio 1 I was taken aback. It wasn't quite Joan Collins wading through the urine and used needles outside Key 103, but I expected the greatest radio station in the world to be a bit more, well, impressive. In late 2012 Radio 1 moves to its new home at the very top of London's Broadcasting House, the new studios looking down swanky Regent Street in one direction and up towards Regent's Park in the other. But back then it was on a very anonymous corner of Great Portland Street, with just a few cafés and a bookmaker's over the road. There was nothing to suggest this was Radio 1; the sign on the door just read 'BBC Yalding House'.

The reception was small, and as I waited there was a huge bustle of DJs, staff, guests and record-company pluggers constantly coming in and out. Then it hit me: it didn't look like much, but this was a different level.

Once I was in the studio I realised that, despite having worked in radio for years, I was woefully inexperienced when it came to personality radio. All I had ever done was introduce records with fairly minimal chat, and it quickly became clear that I had nothing else to offer. I didn't know what to say or how to be entertaining. Radio 1 was about so much more than just playing a list of songs and reading the weather. I could do very tight music radio, in a strict format, but more was required here.

A guy called Fergus Dudley, who now works at Radio 2 and 6 Music, was overseeing my try-out. When I finished I looked at him with fear and trepidation.

'That wasn't very good, was it?' he said. 'Do you want to come back in next week and give it another go?'

It wasn't his honest appraisal of my performance that shocked me; it was the fact that he was willing to give me another chance.

I practised as much as I could over the following week, but when I went back I was equally bad. Just by looking at Fergus's face I knew that this was not what Radio 1 was after.

When a new boss, Lorna Clarke, started at the station I thought I should give it another go as she didn't know my history with the dreadful try-outs.

So I started sending her new, and what I considered to be better, demos. Again I was knocked back.

One day, though, I got a call from Simon Willis, asking me to a meeting with Lorna. I met them for drinks in a private members' bar in Dean Street, having spent a good hour having a mini panic attack and sweating profusely. When I am nervous I don't pace around, I don't bite my nails, I sweat. Not just a little bit: I'm talking buckets.

I was also in my phase of going on strange diets and trying to dress like a pop star, so I was wearing drawstring trousers and probably a shirt with a dragon on it. I used to watch *Top of the Pops* and try to copy what Jamie Theakston wore, but never quite got it right.

As I turned up looking like 911's sweaty brother, I was trying to work out why Lorna and Simon wanted to meet me: I had been rejected by Radio 1 so many times.

We sat down and had a drink, small talk was talked and I looked around the room regularly pointing out how 'this is nice, isn't it?'.

All of a sudden Lorna leaned forward and then paused just as she was about to speak. I instinctively leaned forward to listen. Then she said, 'I know it's been a while and you've sent loads and loads of demos in to us, but we think it's time [pause] to offer you a job.'

For a couple of seconds I couldn't breathe. I really thought I would pass out. I thought I was smiling but I obviously wasn't because Lorna and Simon were looking increasingly concerned.

Finally I started to breathe and a grin spread across my face. The two of them smiled too, probably through relief that they hadn't killed me.

Looking back now, I realise that Lorna was truly ahead of her time. She had just done the classic *X Factor* 'is it good news or bad news?' pause, and *The X Factor* hadn't even been invented.

I don't know what I was expecting her to say, but being

offered a job had not entered my head. I was euphoric, and I don't think I've had a feeling like that since. So many things were whirring around my head and I wanted to phone every single person I knew and tell them.

Lorna kindly fed me some cocktails and then booked me a taxi home. In the car I phoned my mum to tell her the news and we both started crying. She had spent all those years listening to me doing my little DJ shows and pretending to be on Radio 1, and now it was actually happening.

I was also stupidly excited about having a paid-for car ferrying me home. I'd never had that kind of treatment before. I remember sticking my head out of the window of the cab and shouting 'AAAARGH!' at passers-by on Piccadilly Circus.

When I got home I rang all of my friends, then sat for hours staring into space, totally overwhelmed. I barely slept, but the next day I had so much extra energy because I was totally buzzing. After all those years of being told no, I'd finally got the yes I had been praying for, and it was worth the wait. You have no idea how much this meant to me.

My first show was awful. It was September 1998, and I remember opening up the microphone for the first link as my

Me and my mum Sandra. Look at that stunning polka-dot creation.

Me on holiday in Barry Island with my nan. And a monkey.

Rocking the bowl hair.

In my Crestwood school
uniform. Nice hair.

A trophy that I won on
BBC Radio Solent for
my chart knowledge. So
exciting I fell asleep.

I actually look like I'm in *Phoenix Nights*. Everyone loves a hottie with his own mobile disco.

Publicity shot for my first agent in London. Yes, I am wearing make-up. Moonface!

Look, I'm pretending to mix!

See? Me and Chris Moyles are friends.

Me and my long-suffering flatmate Fraser.

I miss Jo Whiley.

Glastonbury. I wasn't a fan. In the background: it's the One That Doesn't Speak!

Failing at the festival look at the Big Weekend in Preston.

On the main stage at the Hackney Weekend in 2012, introducing Jessie J.

mouth went dry. I'd been on air countless times before, but this felt different because listeners could hear me all across the country. It kept going through my head that people in Northern Ireland and Scotland and some places I'd never even been to could hear me. There were potentially millions of people listening to me rambling away. Although maybe not at four o'clock in the morning.

On commercial radio you're pretty much told what to say, within reason, but at Radio 1 they want your personality to shine. At that time I didn't really have a radio personality. I had some meetings before the first show and they asked me what I wanted to do, which was all new because I was used to being told what to do rather than expected to have ideas. To be given the chance to create my own show was totally alien to me. I had a blank canvas but no idea what I wanted to put on it.

I wouldn't say that my first show was technically bad, I just had no idea how to fill the time between songs. So I did what any DJ would do and read out the Radio 1 phone number, probably around 543 times. Despite that, hardly anyone phoned in. Back then there was no Twitter or Facebook, email was relatively new and nobody texted, so I was reliant on phone calls. They weren't forthcoming, which made me worry even more that I was doing a crap job.

These days, if I talk about something on the radio I get immediate feedback through text messages and social networks, and listeners never leave you in any doubt as to whether or not something is working.

As soon as I have said something on Radio 1 the text console will start filling with messages commenting on what the audience has just heard. A general cross-section will look something like this:

07********* Hi Scott, please play Call Me Maybe. Izzy xxxx

07********* U R gay

07********* Just crashed my car laughing. That was the funniest thing I've ever heard in my life. Morgan off of Darlington

07********* My ears are bleeding. This is shit.

07********* Poor it over my kumquats LOL x

07********* Legend ☺

07********* That was hilarious. Olivia x

07********* You are shit.

07********* TELL BECCY SHE IZ FIT.

07********* Hi Steve, love the show, please play Wings for Des in Durham.

07********* Scott – can you say hi to me and Ruthie? Love you bye x

07*********   Are you gay? If you are, just say yes or no
     to Karl in Kent.
07*********   Unsubscribe


Thousands of texts will come in during every show and
they really help me gauge how gay I am, whether or not I'm
a legend, how many listeners' ears are bleeding, and how fit
they think Beccy is today. When we did a stupid feature on
my afternoon show, where my assistant producer Beccy
rapped along to songs badly in a West Country accent,
#beccyraps was the number-one trending topic worldwide on
Twitter for three days in a row. That gave us conclusive proof
that either people really loved it or they really wanted to tell
people how much they hated it.

But back when I started out there was no way of knowing
what people did and didn't like, apart from speaking to them,
so you just followed your instincts and hoped for the best.
I've still got a tape of myself from when I did the *Top of the
Pops* radio show on a Sunday afternoon, and there's a part
where I say, 'If you'd like to fax in about anything we're talking about, please do.' Fax?


My dad got up especially early to listen to my first Radio 1
show and when I had finished I found a message on my

answerphone from him. He was in tears, saying how proud he was. When I called him back he had managed to compose himself and told me that I sounded nervous and like I didn't really know what I was doing. I appreciated that because he was right.

A few days later, something happened that would change my career for ever. I was presenting my fourth show on the station, and it was coming to the end. Most of the last hour had been me telling the listeners that Zoë Ball was coming up at half six and what she had on her show.

A guy had just turned up in reception to pick me up, because I'd agreed to go to France after my show to film an advert for a hypermarket promoting booze cruises. Don't ask.

Just after the security guard had called the studio to tell me the booze-cruise man had arrived and was waiting in his car, I got another phone call.

Zoë Ball was sick. She wasn't coming in. Would I be up for presenting her show?

This was my fourth day. They wanted me to do the Radio 1 Breakfast Show. I was so out of my depth it wasn't even funny.

I was told to think about it for a few minutes. I went outside and took some deep breaths of fresh London air, thought about the task in hand, started sweating profusely, marched back in and told them I'd do it.

I started the show, did a quick link and played a song. The phone in the studio rang. The producer handed me the phone. Was this the boss telling me I was doing a great job? It was security.

'Hello Scott, there's a man here wants to take you on a booze cruise.'

'I'm a bit busy, he'll have to wait till after the Breakfast Show.'

'He's quite insistent. Shall I tell him you'll be five minutes?'

There was already a lot of pre-prepared content for the show and I talked about things that had been touched on earlier in the week and gave updates. I was handed sheets with showbiz stories and facts and figures on them. Zoë had a great team of people who supported me and helped when I looked like I was floundering. It was terrifying but turned out to be a blessing, because ever since then I've covered the slot whenever anyone is unwell or on holiday. I'm not sure that would have happened if I hadn't been given a chance that day and taken it.

Finally, when the show was over the booze-cruise man called the studio in a panic. I had to come. Now!

The advert was truly awful. I had to walk around a hypermarket picking up baguettes and bottles of wine, saying, 'It's less than half the price of the UK', while all around me were French people looking rather bemused. As I travelled back through the Channel Tunnel I wondered if I would have more days as random as this one.

Most of the Radio 1 DJs were really welcoming, but when I first joined I found Chris Moyles quite hard. Whenever he mentioned me on air he would mimic me in a silly camp voice. To start with I ignored it, but the longer it went on the more annoying it got, so I decided to confront him one day. He was mortified that I had been upset. He apologised, and since then we've got on really well. I've got a lot of respect for him, both as a person and as a broadcaster. On a good day nobody can beat Chris Moyles on the radio.

I'll never forget how much Zoë Ball took me under her wing when I first joined the station. I was scared to death and didn't know anyone. On one of my first days she left me a voicemail message inviting me out with her and some of the other Radio 1 people that night. Zoë really went out of her way to make me feel comfortable, even though she didn't know me. I'll always be grateful for that. I used to go and hang out in the studio while she was doing the Breakfast Show, just to watch how she worked. She helped me to get to know other people and made my early days so much easier.

## THINGS I HAVE LEARNED

### #11: I'm not very good at being gay

I'd been at Radio 1 for a few years when I decided it was time to come out publicly. It was 2001 and I was still on early mornings so not that many people knew me, but I felt it was something I wanted to do.

Paul Simpson, Radio 1's head of press at the time, advised me to do an interview with the *Guardian*. They wrote a thoughtful piece without sensationalising it and a couple of the tabloids picked up on the story, but it wasn't big news.

I'm lucky that I haven't been labelled too much in my career. I'm not ashamed of my sexuality in any way, I just don't want to be defined by it. As far as my family are concerned I am the son who just happens to be gay, just as in my mind I am a radio DJ who just happens to be gay.

I always remember the late Kevin Greening being 'the gay DJ' in the press. Kevin was a fantastic broadcaster, so why does it matter that he was gay? Chris Moyles is never 'the straight Radio 1 DJ'.

It annoys me that some people think you should be outrageously camp if you're homosexual and in the public eye.

Here is a conversation I regularly have with people at DJ gigs:

Drunk girl: Hey, you're not *gay*!

Me: Er, yes I am.

Drunk girl: But you don't *sound* gay!

I guess I'm not a very good gay if you are basing it on stereotypes, which many people do. Not only do I not 'sound' gay, I have fairly bad fashion sense, I have no idea about home furnishings and I only go to the gym because I feel I should, not to get super hench. I do have an unashamed love of pop music, though, if that counts.

There are many people like me, who just like to go about their daily lives without shouting about how gay they are every five minutes. Some of them will be reading this book now.

I didn't buy a house until I worked at Radio 1 because I never knew if I'd be moving somewhere else for another job.

The first flat I bought was a little place in Islington and I was thrilled to actually own somewhere, to be able to paint the walls whatever colours I wanted and put nails in them without worrying about losing my deposit, which had happened to me several times over the years.

I only stayed in Islington for a year, but it got me on the ladder and gave me a bit of stability. The second place I bought was in Hackney, and I went to see it on a really sunny day, which is always a mistake: a sunny day makes any area look nice, no matter how rough it is.

Sun streamed through the windows of this beautiful loft conversion as the estate agent told me what an amazing, sought-after area it was, and I took his word for it. I was working so much that I just wanted a base with room to move around, and I thought that as long as I could get into town easily and the flat was nice, that would be enough for me. Plus it was a real bargain. I couldn't believe how cheap it was!

The day I packed up all of my stuff and moved in was really exciting. But my excitement soon turned to terror when, a few days later, I found out that the road I had moved to was affectionately named Murder Mile due to its high crime rate and the number of shootings that go on around there. This wasn't as ideal as the estate agent had led me to believe. It didn't help that every other person I met knew someone who had been attacked around that area. One guy had even been shot at. Speaking to some other friends, they assured me that things like that are very rare and it probably wasn't as bad as people were making out.

As I was working what were known as 'unsociable hours' the BBC used to send a car to pick me up at three o'clock every morning. They were usually pretty nice cabs and I'd often have a nap in the back on the way to work. One day I was running a bit late, and by the time I got downstairs the driver had been carjacked. The taxi company refused ever to go there again.

I had a BMW by this time, and I kept it in a compound that was surrounded by a wire fence. As soon as I drove in there and the gate shut behind me I felt pretty safe. The road leading up to the compound was really narrow, but it was still a two-way street. One day as I was driving home I accidentally nudged the wheel of a parked car. I barely touched it, but unfortunately for me there were four massive guys sitting in the car and they weren't happy. I apologised but the driver got out and started threatening me, telling me to get out because he wanted to 'talk to me'. Remembering all the horror stories, I put my foot down and sped off as quickly as I could. When I looked in my rear-view mirror I could see him getting back in his car, ready to come after me. It was getting dark, so I quickly parked up, slid down in my seat and hid. This was something I had only seen on TV and I was shitting myself. After he had gone zooming past I drove as fast as I could to the compound, thinking he could find me at any minute. Thankfully, I got through the gates to safety, and didn't see them again.

Nowadays, much of that area has got a lot better. I even saw a TV programme the other day about how, since I moved out, my old area is one of the top five coolest places to live. Typical.

# FREQUENTLY ASKED QUESTIONS

## #3: Is your flatmate your boyfriend?

The only good thing about living in that flat was how Fraser, my flatmate, and I became such good friends. Some people think when I talk about 'my flatmate' it's some kind of euphemism; it's not. Fraser and I met through Jon and Robbie, twins who are two of my closest mates. He needed somewhere to stay, I told him he could live with me, and he's never left.

Fraser has been through everything with me, both good and bad, and is incredibly loyal and generous – he'd do anything for you. Or for me, anyway.

A few years ago he was keen to break into stand-up comedy, but had the small handicap of not being particularly funny. He famously lasted sixteen seconds at the Comedy Store's Gong Night before being hauled off the stage.

He became known on my show as My Flatmate the Comedian, and we set him up with some more shows. To be fair, he did get a lot better and even went on to do shows at the Edinburgh Festival.

Fraser is one of those people who believes he can do anything, which I admire because I can be a massive pessimist. Even now, at the age of thirty-two, he still thinks he could be a spaceman or a spy.

He did actually apply to MI5 and got through all the tests, but then they turned him down. Fraser reckons it was because he lives with me and I'm too much of a security risk. He has a perfectly good and well-paid job as the head of planning at an advertising agency, but he will always be a frustrated spy.

We've lived together in Hackney, Shepherd's Bush, Kentish Town and now Crouch End. His girlfriend Kirsty and my boyfriend Brad also live with us now.

Fraser and Kirsty are buying a house together, though, so soon Fraser and I will live apart for the first time in eleven years. We both know it has to happen, but when it does it's going to be really strange, and a bit sad, to be honest.

## CHAPTER 4

# I Am a C****

Shortly after I joined the station I went to my first Radio 1 event. All the producers and DJs got a coach from central London to Cardiff, and I was so nervous I took my good mate Neil with me so I'd have someone to talk to. I'd only been there about a week and no one really knew who I was. I didn't want the awkwardness of having to sit on the bus on my own. I would have felt like the unpopular kid at school.

I felt so proud to be there, but when I tried to get into the event the bouncer refused me entry. I was just about to walk away in shame when the big boss, Andy Parfitt, controller of Radio 1, strolled past and told security to let me in. 'He's a Radio 1 DJ,' he said.

That was the first time I'd ever heard someone call me that. It felt pretty good.

The bouncer stared at me for a couple of seconds, gave me a look that said 'never heard of ya' and let me through.

## THINGS I HAVE LEARNED

### #12: *I am a c\*nt*

Within two weeks of joining Radio 1 I was asked to become a presenter on *Top of the Pops*, which was the biggest music show on TV at the time and every single pop star, no matter how big, appeared on it.

TV was never something I'd thought about before because, despite having my dream job, I still wasn't that confident. But because I was quite young and had awful spiky hair I had the right look. I modelled my hair on Scott from the band Five, and it involved twisting my hair into spikes with strong gel. You can see why they were so keen to have me on the show.

On my first day I headed down to the Elstree studios in Borehamwood – again not a glamorous location for such a huge show.

The great thing about Elstree was the fact that it wasn't just *Top of the Pops* that was filmed there: there was also *EastEnders*. I only realised this on the first day when I was in the canteen, standing with my tray waiting for some apple crumble and custard. All of a sudden I heard the voice.

'All right darlin'!' It was Barbara Windsor, waving to me across the room.

'Hi!' I replied, waving back enthusiastically.

It was only then that I noticed that the person standing next to me was Steve McFadden and she was waving at him. I pretended that I wasn't waving and simply brushing my spiky hair with my hands. I think I got away with it too.

For some reason the *EastEnders* stars have that kind of fame where you already think you know them. I'd often say 'Hi' to Barry in the corridor and expect him to know who I was.

Despite the distraction of Peggy Mitchell in the canteen, I was terrified by what I was about to do. On the radio I felt fine, being in a little box on my own where no one could see me, but here I would be seen and judged not only for how I sounded but how I looked.

When showtime approached I had gone beyond scared. Just before I did my first link I rushed to the toilets to be sick. I had never done this. I had no idea what I was doing. I was worried that my panic attacks would return because I had put myself under so much pressure.

I hadn't had any TV-presenting experience and my first go at it was *Top of the Pops*! As a massive camera swung towards me I froze. Then my voice shot up about ten octaves and I screeched, 'It's still number one. It's *Top of the Pops!'* into my microphone. The audience screamed their delight; they had never heard a man speak in such a high voice before.

There was a pub in Elstree studios and, because there's nothing else around, everyone used to head there straight after the show. I had a few drinks to celebrate getting through my first go at TV presenting. The *EastEnders* actors would also come in after a long day filming, and you'd also see extras from *Holby City*, occasionally still wearing blood-soaked bandages. It was brilliantly absurd – you'd see Dot Cotton having a glass of wine with one of the Manic Street Preachers, or Pat Butcher having a G&T with H from Steps. Every time you went into that bar it was like a weird dream.

Being on the *Top of the Pops* team meant I had to interview all of the guests for spin-off shows. I interviewed Eminem for the first show, which was horrendous. He really didn't want to be there. I was smiling at him to try to perk him up, but he was having none of it. In the end it just looked like a miserable bloke and a man grinning inanely were attempting to have a conversation and failing.

But at least he didn't walk out. The only person who ever did that to me was Brian Molko from Placebo. I asked him why the *NME* hated him so much as they were always slagging him off. And he got up and flounced off. There is no other way of saying it: he didn't storm out, he flounced off.

Ricky Martin was also a bit awkward to interview. He was a really nice guy, but he was obsessed with looking the absolute best he could on TV. He wore loads of make-up and demanded that all these special lenses and gels were put on the cameras to make the lighting as flattering to him as possible. There was one orange-coloured gel that was his absolute favourite, which was once referred to as 'bastard amber gel' by a cameraman because it's so fierce. As a result of that gel he looked amazing on screen, because the type of make-up he was wearing made it seem like he was almost in soft focus, whereas I was so pale the gel made me look green. I still have it on video: he looks like he's in heaven; I look like I'm about to puke.

My confidence wasn't helped when I had to interview Oasis. I'd met them before, and chatted to them briefly, so I thought that might be a bit of an in. They were absolutely huge at the time and renowned for being outspoken. Their radio plugger took me over to Liam and said to him, 'You remember Scott, don't you? You've met him before.' Liam stood there, looked me up and down and went, 'Yeah, he's a cunt.'

# THINGS I HAVE LEARNED

## #13: *When warming up for Lady Gaga there are only two things you need to remember*

It's May 2011 and I am in Carlisle. I am on the stage in front of a packed Big Weekend audience who are waiting to see the headliner, Lady Gaga. The anticipation in the crowd is huge. I have been asked to do the warm-up DJ set which will also be screened live on TV to millions of people. I've been told to play for half an hour and things are going well. When Gaga is ready to appear I'll see a countdown clock on the big screen; this will signal her arrival is imminent so I can finish the set and count down to her coming on stage.

The crowd are loving it, I'm playing massive tunes and inserting clips of Lady Gaga saying things like, 'I'll be with you soon.' The excitement is building. It's nearly time.

It is at that moment that I learn the first rule of warming up for Lady Gaga:

*Never, ever slice your hand open and spray blood everywhere.*

Behind me are huge LED screens showing videos, and for some reason I decide to turn around and touch the one nearest to me. I have no idea why I do this. I also have no idea why the screens are razor sharp.

But I do and they are. My finger is sliced open by the

screen, and it immediately begins bleeding extremely heavily. I remember the cameras are on me and this is all going out live on TV, so I attempt to keep my hand out of sight so no one can see the blood dripping onto the decks.

I decide I need help. I am grinning to cover the pain and embarrassment but this is making me look slightly unhinged.

'Beccy!' I shout to my assistant producer.

Beccy catches my eye and sees me grinning. She grins back in an equally unhinged manner and gives me the thumbs up.

'*Beccy!*' I shout again.

Beccy glances down and her inane grin quickly disappears when she sees the blood gushing from my hand. She looks back up at my face. I am now grinning like someone from a horror movie who is about to kill everyone on the screen.

I mouth the word 'Help' and she quickly runs off, I hope in the direction of help.

I have been playing for half an hour and any second now the countdown clock will appear on the big screen that has cost me so much of my blood.

I hold my finger against my jeans as firmly as I can to try to stop the flow of blood and attempt to DJ with one hand. I glance at the crowd and notice someone in the front row looking at me, concerned. I glance down to see my blood-soaked jeans and realise it looks like I have been shot in the leg.

I grin back at the member of the audience. They now look even more concerned.

I notice the time. Gaga is late. Where is she? It is now that I learn the second rule for warming up for Lady Gaga: *always bring more music than you need.*

I was told it would be half an hour. I am starting to run out of songs.

Beccy returns from the St John Ambulance people with some plasters.

I put a plaster on and finally the screen flashes up '00:01:00'. The clock starts to count down. With my good hand I raise the microphone to my mouth and shout, 'One minute to Lady Gaga!'

The crowd goes berserk. I have survived blood-loss and a potential music shortage but she is nearly on stage. I am grinning maniacally again, this time with relief.

I hear Beccy shout, 'Scott!'

I see her point to the big screen. The countdown clock has disappeared. It was a false alarm. I sense the mood of the crowd shift. They're not happy.

I try to change the atmosphere and switch to the next track, quickly remembering I am running very low on music.

Blood is now oozing through the plaster and dripping everywhere again.

I have one song left. If she doesn't hurry up I will be on to the last track.

I look at the CD case to see what the song is.

It is 'The Hokey Cokey'. I remember we brought the CD with us for a possible radio feature and now this is the only music I have left to play before Lady Gaga, the world's biggest pop star, comes on stage.

Blood is now covering most of my arm and I try to imagine whether or not 'The Hokey Cokey' would be a good song for Lady Gaga to come on stage to.

My face is now aching from my crazed expression and I put the CD in the machine.

I decide we will change the lyrics to 'Knees bend, arm stretch, Ga Ga Ga' and I'll get the crowd to sing along.

Suddenly I hear a scream from the audience. The countdown clock has come back on.

'One minute to Lady Gaga,' I squeal over the microphone.

The clock stays counting down.

'5-4-3-2-1' we all chant together.

Lady Gaga arrives on stage in a coffin.

I nearly pass out.

## CHAPTER 5

# A Very Dark Place

You might think this would have been the best time of my life, having secured the dream I'd been chasing since I was a child. But something awful happened, and it turned my world upside down.

I love Wales, and in 2000 when on a visit with some friends I met a brilliant guy called Mitch. He was the funniest, most handsome bloke, with the loveliest family. The kind of person everyone enjoys being around, and who would light up even the dullest of events or conversations. Things moved so fast that he soon came to live with me in London. About ten months after we got together we went to Miami for two weeks, and it was one of the best holidays I've ever been on.

The night after we got back from our holiday it was the Brit

Awards. I was going along to do my radio show backstage, and he went off to a party with some friends. We arranged to meet up after the show.

The Brits went well and I was on a real high. When I finished I kept calling Mitch but I couldn't get hold of him, so I assumed he was having a good time and would call me back once he picked up my messages.

I headed back to the hotel we were staying at to wait for him there. I stayed up for a couple of hours and called a few more times, but I was so tired I eventually fell asleep.

I was woken up by a phone call. It was the kind of call everyone dreads. The police were waiting in reception and wanted to talk to me. Something bad had happened, but I didn't know what. I threw my clothes on and rushed downstairs.

When I got to reception, a policeman took me aside. I just wanted him to tell me what had happened, but it seemed to take an age before he finally got the words out. Mitch had died.

Everything stopped. I felt a huge pain in my stomach and I couldn't hear anything that was being said. I just stood staring at the policeman in disbelief, not taking in what he was telling me. The policeman tried to explain what had happened but I wasn't really listening. I just heard something about drugs and an accident. Nothing was making sense, it felt like my whole life had fallen apart in an instant. I went back to the room, packed my stuff and checked out of the hotel.

I met up with my friend Neil, but was in such a state of shock that I didn't know what to do with myself. We headed for breakfast at McDonald's, but I could only stare at the wall. I'd explained what had happened over the phone and I think I just wanted some company and to pretend that it wasn't real. I acted as normally as I could, but if Neil tried to talk about it I'd change the subject and ramble on about something inane for a few minutes before going silent again.

I was supposed to be on air that afternoon, to do the *Top of the Pops* radio show, but I could hardly think, never mind speak. I didn't know what to do. I couldn't face telling anyone at work what had happened so I turned up at Radio 1 and went ahead with the show, trying to block out anything to do with Mitch as if I was attempting to convince myself that it hadn't happened.

After the show I went home, sat on the sofa and sobbed for hours. Once the enormity of what had happened hit me I was overwhelmed, totally heartbroken, and didn't know how to deal with my grief. I'm not sure if I dealt with it at all, to be honest.

It wasn't as if Mitch had been ill; it just came out of nowhere. I couldn't understand how he could be there one day and gone the next. At that point, all of my grandparents were still alive so I'd never experienced death before, and I had no idea how to handle it.

Once I finally managed to explain to my bosses what had happened they gave me some time off and I went to stay with Neil in Birmingham for a week. I had to get away from London and have some space to try to work things out.

To add to all this, the Radio 1 press office kept calling me, saying that the papers had got hold of the story and were planning to run something. I didn't make any comment, so every night I would panic about what I would wake up to the next day. I didn't want them to cheapen something that was so important to me, or to show Mitch in a bad light. I was worried everything would be sensationalised, because at that point I wasn't publicly out. All my friends and family knew that I was gay, but it wasn't something I had talked about on the radio or in the press because I'd never felt the need.

I was really close to Mitch's family and so I was concerned about how any kind of story would affect them. I was even nervous about going to the funeral in case any press were there. This was such a sad loss and I just wanted the family to be able to grieve; I couldn't bear the thought of them being hurt any more than they had been already. In the end the papers did run something, but it was thankfully only a small piece. They called Mitch my friend, and I was relieved that it wasn't a big story as the family had been through such an awful time. The last thing in the world they deserved was that.

It took me a long time to get over his death. I still think about Mitch all the time, and I miss him a lot. He was so young and it seems unfair that he died in such a horrible way. People may judge because he was at a party and there were drugs involved, but he wasn't the kind of guy who did stupid things. He was lovely and caring and kind, and one of the best friends I've ever had.

The pressure of everything got too much for me over the next few months. I returned to work and tried to get things back to normal, but they weren't normal. I missed Mitch terribly, and it's fair to say my drinking got out of control for a while.

I worked on the early shift for a total of five years, and during that time I hardly ever saw daylight. I think that really got to me and contributed to my feeling low. I used to have to go to bed at eight or nine so I could get up at three in the morning, which totally messed up my body clock. I lost myself for quite a long time and, following Mitch's death, didn't want to face any kind of reality.

Many mornings I would get home after my shift and start

drinking. I'd be pissed by the time *This Morning* came on. I remember one day trying to phone in to their quiz, You Say, We Pay. Unsurprisingly, I wasn't put through.

Things escalated very quickly. I could easily get through a bottle of spirits a day, no problem. When *This Morning* finished I would start watching the shopping channels and order loads of stuff I didn't need. I lost count of the number of times I'd get home from work and find that things I couldn't remember buying had been delivered. I ended up with so much crap, including a twenty-four-piece knife set, an exercise bike and a barrel of industrial carpet cleaner. My flat had no carpets; there were wooden floors.

Another highlight was when I called up an evangelical radio station in America and went live on air, where they were claiming that being gay is wrong. I joined in the debate and was on the phone for a good half an hour. I was so bored being on my own all day that I would do anything to amuse myself. I was also incredibly lonely: since Mitch, I didn't know what to do.

By now, Fraser had moved in with me. He'd come home from work at five o'clock and I would still be drinking. We went on a break to Prague and brought back a load of booze, and I managed to get through the whole lot in one day. Fraser kept telling me I had to sort myself out and stop the boozing, but it had become a habit that was so hard to get out of.

I was also suffering from my nerves again. My panic attacks returned, and I really thought the drinking would help calm me down. But in fact it was doing exactly the opposite. It's a vicious circle: you feel down, so you drink to feel better. You feel really low the day after drinking, and repeat.

It was as if I was discovering the teenage years I never had, but to the extreme. Because I was working in radio from such a young age I didn't ever do the whole teenage 'going away with your mates on holiday to Magaluf and getting hammered for two weeks' thing. I had fun, but not the kind of fun that other teenagers were having.

I discovered clubbing really late, and I started going to Ibiza for holidays or jumping in the car and going up to Birmingham for nights out with Neil. All too often I had that awful experience of sitting in your mate's flat at nine o'clock in the morning, wondering if it would be better to go to bed or have another drink. There is nothing worse than walking out of a club when the sun's coming up and the birds are tweeting, and you already know you're going to feel like hell. The idea of doing that now fills me with absolute horror, but back then it just felt like that was what I wanted to do. I was a bit lost; I didn't really stop and take in what had happened.

I got really friendly with some people at work and we often used to go out drinking together. One particularly bad period was the summer of 2002. Japan and South Korea hosted the

World Cup, and because of the time difference loads of pubs were opening super-early so that people could go and watch the matches.

The team and I used to finish work at seven and go straight to the Albany, a pub near work, where we'd have a full English breakfast and then order bottle upon bottle of white wine. There's no way I could do that now, but drinking was something I was very good at in my twenties.

We would still be there in the late afternoon. I remember that once, sitting at the end of a table, I fell off my stool. I keeled over because I was so drunk I couldn't sit up straight any more. Someone had to put me in a taxi home and I slept until I had to get up for my show, at three in the morning, and I felt absolutely fine. My body seemed to be able to handle the drink okay, so there was never a big incentive to stop.

My drinking did, however, become a bit of a nightmare for my downstairs neighbours. If I came home pissed I would regularly find myself standing in their living room, having gone into the wrong flat. Because we were all in the same block, and all the doors looked alike, I'd often miss the last flight of stairs and walk into their flat instead. God knows why they didn't lock their doors. As I was all over the place it would take me a while to work out where I was.

The first time I wandered in it really freaked them out, but after the third time they got used to it. They'd turn me around and point me in the right direction, and I'd stagger upstairs and fall into bed.

Another time, we'd all been out and got hammered and Justin Timberlake was coming on the Breakfast Show, which I was covering for the usual host. My producer had to take Justin aside before the show and apologise in case the studio smelt of alcohol because we were all so hungover. He shrugged it off, but it wasn't exactly professional of us and I still cringe when I think about it.

On a good work day I would come home straight after work, sleep from eight until around midday, and then sit around watching TV and paying bills or whatever while tucking into some wine. If I had friends over, or if Fraser came home after having been out for a few drinks, I'd open another bottle of wine. I wouldn't go to bed until around eleven or midnight. I'd have a few hours' sleep and then be back at work. Sleeping in two shifts like this meant that I was always knackered.

Eventually, I got so fed up of feeling hungover and tired that I became a bit of a recluse and would avoid seeing people unless I had to. One winter I barely saw any daylight; I just wanted to hide away. I used my tiredness as an excuse and stayed in the flat all the time I wasn't at work, thinking too much and wondering how I was going to sort myself out.

This went on for what seemed like an eternity. I managed

to curb the everyday drinking, but the binge drinking stayed with me. Every time I found myself in a pub or at a party I didn't know when to stop, and would always be the most drunk person there.

Chris Moyles used to host regular karaoke nights, and in 2006 he held one at Dundee University during the Radio 1 Big Weekend. All of the other Radio 1 DJs were there and I got absolutely smashed on wine. I do love white wine, as is well known, but I believe it is the juice of evilness. It can turn people into someone they really don't want to be. I was singing a duet with Jo Whiley when I fell over a speaker and had to be helped out. I woke up the next morning full of self-loathing, and when I checked my phone I had loads of messages from people going, 'God, you were off it last night!' That's the worst thing: when you know you made a complete tit of yourself. In your mind you convince yourself that you were fine and no one really noticed how wasted you were, but when you're faced with the evidence there's no ignoring it. I got used to making jokes about what a pisshead I was while dying inside and promising myself I would never do it again.

It wasn't just at home or in the pub that the drinking was a problem, it was every time I went anywhere. I agreed to DJ at Fraser's sister Joanne's wedding. Booking me for a late slot back then was not a good idea. I drank champagne all night so I was pissed quite early, and when my ten o'clock slot rolled around I was so drunk I spilt a bottle of champagne all over the DJ equipment. Fraser looked after me and cleaned up the mess. We managed to save the equipment, but only just. The last song I played before I was escorted from the DJ booth was the James Blunt song about three wise men. Who wants to hear that at a wedding? In fact, who wants to hear that ever?

I was helped out and someone had to put on an iPod so everyone could dance for the rest of the evening. I felt so terrible about it that I later made a public apology on air during the chart show. Even though Fraser's family laugh about it now, it's one of those things I'm not sure I'll ever forgive myself for. I guess in some ways it made Joanne's wedding more memorable, but not in the way it should have been.

Poor Fraser had to put up with a lot of my drinking, and I did so many embarrassing things. We went on a really lovely holiday to South Africa and I promised myself that I wouldn't do what I always did, getting completely wrecked on the first night and then feeling awful for days. But of course the first-night excitement kicked in as soon as we arrived and I got plastered. I was so pissed that I started texting Fearne Cotton, Davina McCall and Lorraine Kelly and asking what kind of knickers they were wearing. I woke up the next day feeling like hell and swore off booze for ever. But by the evening we were back on it.

The next evening Fraser and I were having drinks at the bar when a couple came up and introduced themselves to us. They recognised me, and we ended up spending the evening chatting and had quite a laugh. I've never really been one for making holiday friends but after that, every time we saw them, the couple would insist we had drinks or join them for dinner.

It felt rude to say no, but it's an awkward position to be put in. They were lovely people, but we wanted to do our own thing and whenever we saw them the more time they wanted to spend with us. It just got too much.

In the end, to get away from them, we told them that we were planning to travel around for a while and we moved to another hotel. They were quizzing us about where because they were planning to do the same thing, so to put them off the scent we lied and told them a totally different area from where we were actually heading, in case they followed us.

The next day, Fraser and I set off, travelling for four hours to a hotel we'd found online. We dumped our stuff and went down for dinner. Only when we were seated, we noticed that the couple from the other hotel were at the next table. It was awful, and so obvious that we'd lied to them about where we were going. We sat at the table in silence. Luckily there were a few other people in the restaurant – it wasn't just us and them – but it still made for one of the most uncomfortable meals of my life.

During the same holiday we stupidly got into the back of a random bloke's car because we decided we wanted to go for a burger. Anyone who's been to South Africa knows that the last thing you want to do out there is get into a car if you're not 100 per cent sure it's a proper taxi. You hear horror stories about tourists being kidnapped or beaten up all the time, so we were incredibly lucky that we got back to the hotel safely. It makes me shudder because literally anything could have happened. When I look back at some of the dodgy situations I've got myself into when I've been drinking, I find it incredible that I haven't ever come to any real harm.

I was a complete disgrace back then. In 2002 I went to the premiere of *Minority Report*, but I'd been on a booze binge beforehand and a result I fell asleep and snored the entire way through. I don't know quite what everyone else in the cinema made of it.

Another time, I went to an event at the St Martin's Lane Hotel. Emma Samms, who had played Fallon in *Dynasty*, was there. We knew each other from a show we had been on – *Celebrity Scissorhands* – and that evening we acted out old scenes from *Dynasty* for the bemused-looking bar staff.

*

My drinking meant that I was making some bad choices when it came to friends and boyfriends. These days I think I'm a really good judge of character, but back then I had a lot to learn. Everything was one big party and I went along for the ride. I was always looking for the next high and trying to live the sort of life I thought a DJ should have.

When I was working at Heart I'd go in, play Simply Red and the Lighthouse Family, then go home again and I wouldn't think about work until the next day. But Radio 1 quickly became all-consuming. I love that it still is, and the fact I'm a part of it is incredible, but when I first joined it was my whole life in a very different way.

I threw myself into it: it was all about celeb bashes and getting trashed and regaling everyone with the stories the next day. I think that back then I ended up with a lot of hangers-on because I was on the radio, not because they liked me. But I couldn't see it at the time. I did get burned a few times, with people only being nice to me because they wanted tickets for gigs or whatever, but thankfully I opened my eyes to it pretty quickly once I sobered up. Now I keep people around me that I've known for ages and can trust. I love meeting new people, but it's rare for me to let someone into my friendship group on a deep level.

Even though I'm in the public eye I'm still quite a private person. I'm at a nice level, where people say 'Hi' if they see me in the street, but the paparazzi aren't camped outside my house. I could never be massively famous; I honestly could not cope with it.

I was feeling very raw for a long time after Mitch died, and dating was the last thing on my mind. I went to a party at Strawberry Moons in central London about a year after he passed away and a guy, Daniel, came up to me and kissed me on the cheek. He handed me his number and asked me to call him.

I texted him later that night because I was really keen, and we arranged to meet in Leicester Square at seven o'clock the following evening. I got my best clothes on and headed to meet him, but then at five to seven I got a text saying, 'Sorry, I can't make it.' I was gutted and was texting him back when someone put their hands over my eyes. It was him. It was such an odd thing to do, and it kind of set the tone for the rest of the relationship. He was younger than me and really into clubbing, but I'd moved out of that phase by then so our interests were totally different. He was a part-time model, super good-looking and very, very confident. Even at this stage my confidence was not high, and I ended up feeling needy and paranoid. I was always worried about where he was and who he was with. He wasn't always nice to me. After what I'd been through I wanted a loving, stable relationship. He was argumentative and didn't appreciate anything I did for him, but I think it was because I was so lonely that I was blinded to how awful he was being. I ended up staying with him for about a year. After we split up I decided that I would never go out with someone who was that good-looking again: it had just made me feel insecure. Dating a model definitely doesn't make you feel the best about yourself.

I decided to have some time to myself after Daniel and I split up, and it was not until months later, while I was out one night, that I met the guy who was to become my next boyfriend. I was in a nightclub in Oxford with Neil and I was feeling a bit sorry for myself, but as soon as he walked in I was like, 'Who's that?' Neil has no qualms about going up to anybody and talking to them, and he gets straight to the point. He went over and quite literally said, 'My friend fancies you.' I went bright red and was not surprised when he said he was straight. He was with a group of girls, and I said to Neil to leave it. Neil knows that when he used to do that it was a massive cringe moment for me. I hated it.

Neil and I were going to Homelands Festival the next day and we had some spare tickets so we gave them to Lee, as the guy was called – actually, he wasn't, but let's call him that – and his mates. We all had a brilliant time and as a result Lee and I became friends. I used to go and visit him and over the course of that summer we became more than friends. I had a great time, we used to see each other a lot and we had loads of fun. I really like him, and he was a decent bloke. The problem was that he was essentially straight, and I think because we got on so well he thought that being with me was what he wanted. He mistook brilliant friendship for love. But he liked girls, and I was never going to win.

I met a lot of people through Lee, though, and if I hadn't met him I wouldn't know some of my close friends now. That includes my friend Jon and his brother Robbie, who are still very close to me and I love to bits. And through them, of course, I met Fraser. So Lee did actually shape a lot of my life, even though I didn't know it at the time.


My drinking is something I am certainly not proud of, and on one occasion it very nearly got me fired.

I had done a radio show backstage at the 2003 Brit Awards and was due to be back on air at four o'clock the next morning. So in retrospect it wasn't a great idea to go to one of the after-show parties.

EMI Records were hosting a party at the Sanderson Hotel and I decided to go along. Kylie and Justin Timberlake, who had done a duet at the Brits, were there, as was Janet Jackson. It was very glamorous and I got a bit over-excited: the drinks were free so I was making the most of it. All of a sudden my friend Tina told me it was two in the morning. I was due on air in two hours. This appeared to be time to leave.

Radio 1 had put me up in a hotel right next to the radio station to make sure I had time to get some proper sleep after the Brits, so I rushed back and went to bed, hoping to grab at least a bit of sleep before I had to present live to the nation.

The next thing I know, I woke up and saw two people in my bedroom. One of them was Lizzie, my producer, and the other was a strange man I had never met.

Lizzie introduced him as the hotel's manager. I hadn't been answering my mobile or the room phone, so Lizzie had got the manager to open the door for her.

She was looking very disappointed. I lay on the bed, slowly coming to, and noticed that she was gesturing with her eyes for me to look downwards. It was at this point that I realised I was wearing the black shirt I had worn to the Brits and absolutely nothing else: before I fell into bed I had somehow managed to remove my pants, but not my shirt. Poor Lizzie was fairly new to Radio 1 and here she was, faced with me half naked and in a right state.

I jumped out of bed and rushed out of the door to do my show, only to be guided back by Lizzie who suggested it would be best if I put my pants and trousers on first.

The good news is that I made it onto the radio on time. The bad news is that I was still completely drunk. When I've had a few drinks I sound stereotypically drunk, slurring like a cartoon character.

My first words were, 'Blur 2, "Song 2". "Scandalous". I've been to the Brits!' It made no sense; I had no idea what I was saying. Lizzie had been so worried about me that, beforehand, she had told me to just play records and not speak because I was slurring so badly. But when she went to get me yet another coffee to sober me up, I opened the mic and started rambling on about the Brits, saying, 'So you know how you have posh seats up the front on the plane and the cheap ones down the back? Well that's what the Britsssshhh wassshhh like.' She came rushing in and said, 'Stop talking and drink your coffee.'

Records were fading out and there were silences where I'd forgotten to fill in. People were pulling onto the hard shoulders of motorways because they were laughing so much. It was the worst show I've ever done. Afterwards, I could barely remember that I'd done the show at all.

I'm still so grateful to Lizzie for looking after me because, looking back, I should have been given the sack. Especially after she'd had to see my wanger. She emigrated to Australia soon afterwards, but tells me it was in no way connected to this incident.

I went home after the show and I cried my eyes out. I realised how stupid I was being. I said to myself, 'What are you doing? You've got the best job in the world and you're massively fucking it up. You're going to be fired today.' I was waiting for the call to come, telling me they were letting me go.

I wanted to try to sleep my hangover off but every time I closed my eyes I'd get panicky. I couldn't eat or drink; all I could do was cry. I sat staring at the phone, waiting for it to ring and for my boss to tell me not to bother coming in the next day. I was full of self-loathing and there was nothing I could do to make myself feel better. I've never been more upset with myself than I was that day.

Pat Connor, my executive producer at the time, was astonishingly sympathetic about it and told everyone they should have taken me off the early shift because I'd been working so late the evening before. Thank God for her. Pat and Lizzie pretty much saved me. That was a dark, dark day.

The horrible thing was that my family were really concerned about me, and I hate to think they were worrying. They didn't outright say 'We think you've got a problem', but there was the odd comment here and there about my drinking, and there were a few family events that I didn't turn up at. I hate letting people down, so those kind of things made me feel even worse about myself.

As time went on, something clicked and I decided enough was enough – I needed to calm down. I cut down massively and because I felt so much better as a result, that encouraged me to carry on looking after myself. I did still have a drink when I went out, but I cut out all the boozing at home and managed to get myself back on track. I don't think I had ever truly dealt with the death of Mitch, but getting out of the alcohol haze and realising I could feel happy without a drink in my hand was a revelation.

Even if booze wasn't involved I still managed to find myself in trouble sometimes. I had a close call at work, about four years into the job, when I didn't turn up for my show at all. I must have been overtired and needed the sleep, as I somehow managed to sleep in until nine in the morning, when I had been due on air at four. I woke up and looked at the clock, and it took me ages to work out what it said. I didn't know if it was nine in the morning or nine at night because I was so disorientated. When I looked at my phone I had sixty-four missed calls.

The thing is, I have no idea how I managed to sleep through my alarms. I had six of them, all in the shape of a mosque, that I'd brought back from Dubai. They were all set to go off at three. They played the azaan, so every single morning they would screech one after the other. This was at the time the UK was invading Afghanistan, and I have no idea what my neighbours must have thought. I'd often sleep with my window open, so they'd get treated to six calls to prayer all kicking off at once. I had to physically get up and turn them off, so that morning I must have turned them all off and gone back to bed. The guy who was on air before me had to fill in. As soon as I became aware of what had happened I had that awful cold feeling inside. I knew I was in big trouble.

The next day I had to go to a scary meeting with the Radio 1 bosses, and I had to take my agent along. They laid it on the line, telling me, 'This is not good enough. You probably want to be looking for another job because we don't think we're going to keep you on when your contract finishes. You're too much of a loose cannon and we can't have that.' From then on I bucked my ideas up. It was the shock I needed to get back on track. I never missed another show.

My breakthrough came when Jamie Theakston decided to take a career break and Radio 1 was looking for a replacement for his Saturday-morning show. It started at ten o'clock, and I did it alongside my early-morning show, so I was working six days a week.

It was a big opportunity, because when you've been doing the early shift for five years you do wonder whether you are ever going to move up through the schedule to daytime. I had almost resigned myself to being on the graveyard shift for ever. I was so grateful to be on at a decent time of day because I felt like I'd been forgotten about. No bosses ever heard me because they weren't up when I was on air and I was in the wilderness. My career was not moving on and, let's be honest, I had hardly helped it along myself in recent times.

The moment I felt relaxed was the absolute key to me finding my voice on radio, if you like. I'd covered other shows over the years, like Zoë Ball's Breakfast Show, but the Saturday-morning show was different. I had a say in the content and I was able to come up with ideas. Having been on the radio since I was sixteen, it was only then that I felt the real me started to shine through. Or rather, a slightly more animated version of myself.

The Saturday-morning show was basically for people with hangovers, including myself sometimes, and I would mess around and have fun.

The fact that I was being more 'out there' and was finding my feet had a knock-on effect with the early shows. I got a lot more confident, and that's when I started to get properly noticed. A guy called Ben Cooper – who was second in command to Andy Parfitt – heard my Saturday-morning shows and really liked what I was doing. He heard something in those shows that other people hadn't, and he identified some potential in me.

Andy recently left the station and Ben became the controller; they are the reason that I've now been on daytime radio for seven years. Ben helped my career at Radio 1 to progress at a time when I didn't think it was going to go anywhere. He took a chance on me and to this day he is a constant source of advice and feedback, and just brilliant to work with. I am so thankful to him for that.

I also cannot thank Andy Parfitt enough for all the help he gave me. I miss his enthusiasm and positivity, and he kept me on air at a time when I probably shouldn't have been because of all the incidents that had happened. If I was him I would have sacked me. But he stuck with me and I'll be eternally grateful.

At around the time I was doing the Saturday shows I started working with a guy called Emlyn Dodd, who is my producer to this day. We've got a ten-year working relationship now and it's like a radio marriage. He's known on the show as 'the one that doesn't speak' because he doesn't like being on air. He's the most creative person I've worked with in all my time in radio. He is constantly full of incredible ideas.

We started working together on the earlies and he helped me to formulate some kind of structure, and we later moved to afternoons together. Every day on the afternoon show he'll come up with new stuff, or how to put a brilliant spin on things, or features that will make the audience laugh. A large amount of my show's popularity is absolutely down to him. He comes up with funny things that people will remember and love, and then I present them in my own style.

We've got the same weird sense of humour and he's easily the best person I've ever worked with. I'm not a diva in any way when it comes to work and I like to think I'm very low maintenance, but the one thing I always ask for when it comes to my shows is that Emlyn stays with me. I realise I may be gushing a bit, but I'm so grateful to be working with him. If he ever leaves me I will find him and kill him.

# CHAPTER 6

# One Night with Laura

In early 2004 I was moved off the early slot and given two weekend shows every Saturday and Sunday afternoon, from one until four.

Moving off earlies and to be living in the same time zone as everyone else came as a huge relief. I found that I had energy to see my friends and even pay my bills, something I had got into the habit of putting off until it was too late. Gone were the days of hiding in the lounge, peeping through the curtains, waiting for the bailiffs to go away; I was a fully functioning member of society again.

Then, having had a taste of daytime radio shows, I was always hopeful that a weekday slot would eventually come up.

Sara Cox was hosting the Drivetime show, and when she was due to go on maternity leave I was asked to step in. It was the slot I'd always wanted to do, so things couldn't have worked out better. It wasn't a full-time position but it was a great start. Emlyn came with me as producer and we now had to come up with some ideas.

# HOW TO CREATE A SONY AWARD-WINNING RADIO SHOW

Everybody has a different way of working and there are no hard and fast rules about what makes good radio, but when I'm asked how we create our show, these are the general principles we follow.

## *The napkin is your friend*

For us, as much as you need headphones you need napkins. Every single idea that has worked well on our radio show has started life on a napkin. There is a lot of talk about creative theory, brainstorms, thought showers, ideas jacuzzis and eureka douches, but if there's no napkin to write it on you'll end up forgetting your idea. I've been told some programmes now use paper or even computers for this, but for me the good old napkin remains king.

## What makes this funny?

We all know that analysing a joke is the first way to kill it, but knowing why something is funny is essential to bringing an idea to life. If Flirt Divert could have worked just by playing out those messages on their own it would have saved a lot of money on presenters' salaries. Unfortunately, while cost-effective, it wouldn't have been half as funny without the chat around the clips. Knowing that made it a hugely successful feature and kept a DJ and his two sidekicks in employment.

## Everyone has a defined role

The reason Emlyn is known as 'the one that doesn't speak' isn't simply because he doesn't want to talk on the radio. And, contrary to rumours, it's not because he has the voice of a six-year-old girl. It's because, when we started working together, DJs on Radio 1 were involving their producers on air a lot, purely because they were lazy. He was horrified that these people the audience didn't know or care about were shouting opinions just to help the DJ, so he took a vow of silence. The theory is that everyone who speaks on the show needs a defined role, so regular listeners know who they are and hopefully care about what they have to say. That's why we each have an on-air character: Chris is the Watford fan with the get-rich-quick schemes who's like someone from *The Inbetweeners*, Beccy is the West Country rapper and I'm the orange moonface who likes wine.

## Work backwards

Some ideas just gradually develop on the radio, and get bigger and bigger. Wherever possible we try to work out what the big end-result of a feature will be before we start. ScottCam, where my house was filled with webcams for a week, with the audience monitoring my every move, seemed to grow from our obsession with a webcam in a zoo to a camera on Beccy's desk to finally my whole house being rigged up. In reality, we had the ScottCam idea first and worked backwards to create the reason why we were doing this. I must point out that the Shaolin monks in my bedroom were not actually planned at any stage, though.

## Don't be afraid to fail

Sometimes things just don't work. Get over it and try something else. It's only by failing that you ever work out how to succeed. That's how I try to make myself feel better, anyway.

## Confound expectations

There is no such thing as 'so bad it's good'. Except perhaps Wing, but she's at least trying to be good. If you're trying to make something bad it will simply suck. Why aim for that? When we started putting the musical together for the Edinburgh Festival in 2009 we thought that even if it was a shambles it would be funny. But it soon became clear that a shambles would just be embarrassing. In the end we somehow created a play people really liked when they weren't expecting much. And that's one of the main reasons it was such a success. That and the fact that I wasn't in it much.

I officially moved to the afternoon slot in June 2004. I was pretty nervous for the first few weeks but I had a great team in Emlyn, Laura Sayers and Mark Chapman, aka Chappers.

One of my favourite items we did was One Night with Laura. Laura was the assistant producer on the show when I first took over.

The whole thing began when Laura's younger sister Mary found her old diaries in their parents' house in York and started ringing her up and reading out embarrassing extracts. Emlyn and I thought it would be hilarious to get Mary to read them out live on air. So every afternoon, at a quarter past five, Mary would phone and regale the nation with stories about boys Laura snogged in her teens and the shameful things she'd done at university. It all felt a bit wrong to start with but it ran for about a year and people absolutely loved it, to the point where it was later made into a book.

As a result of the diaries being read out, we discovered that Laura wasn't very lucky in love. She had put herself out there and dated but had some real disasters.

We decided that the next step would be to do a feature in which we tried to find Laura a boyfriend – and so One Night with Laura was born. It was when *The X Factor* was getting really big and we wanted to do something loosely based on that show. Like *The X Factor*, we toured the country auditioning people, but instead of winning a record contract they would win a date with Laura. It was all very tongue in cheek and we were never expecting to actually find her future husband, but somehow we did!

A big tour bus took us around the country; it was huge, with enormous photos of Laura and me on the side. We often forgot it was so heavily branded, but then we'd look out of the window and wonder why people were pointing, waving, shouting and aiming the occasional 'wanker' sign in our direction. It was certainly a step up from a car with my name written on the side. We'd sleep in the coach at night and feel like proper rock stars, apart from Chappers, who would moan about how uncomfortable it was.

At the auditions the panel consisted of me, Chappers, Laura and, hilariously, Laura's dad. He was brilliant and would grill the potential boyfriends each night. One by one, lads would troop in and try to impress her with their charm and sometimes talents, and one by one they would leave brokenhearted.

People loved watching the auditions and the website got millions of hits in the first seven days: the figures were absolutely huge. Once we got down to the final four contestants the listeners decided who would be voted off each day.

Eventually, Laura's new boyfriend was announced; it was Gareth, a slightly drunk bloke with a strong West Country accent from Chard in Somerset. I think he impressed everyone with his attitude of not really wanting to win. Laura and Gareth went off on their first date to Disneyland Paris with the rest of us tagging along as chaperones.

I mentioned that Laura found her future husband in the competition, but it wasn't Gareth. During the week of the finals, Laura was sneaking off for secret dates with James, the bloke who came fourth!

In 2011 Laura and James got married and I spoke at their wedding, just to let everyone know how the groom won the bride in a competition.

I was gutted when Laura left the show in 2008. She had been fearless and up for anything – and the listeners loved her for it. Over a few years she had become an on-air vigilante, accosting people who don't pick up their dogs' poo; she became a bathroom attendant in the gents' toilet of a local dive pub; she dressed as a man and attempted to get into X-rated clubs; and went shopping on Bond Street dressed as Paris Hilton and asked for free clothes. We sent her to Sainsbury's, where she opened a packet of cereal, poured milk into the packet and then sat on the floor eating it until she was asked to leave. If you suggested something ridiculous to her, she'd do it without thinking twice.

Laura was the assistant producer and as I already had a producer on my show, Emlyn, she needed to move up or risk being stuck in the same job for ever.

She went to work on Fearne Cotton's and Reggie Yates's weekend shows, and now produces Greg James's Drivetime show. She's doing an amazing job and we're still mates, but at times I do miss working with her closely.

Another sad moment was when Chappers left the show. Mark is a brilliant broadcaster and had been presenting the sport and being the sidekick since I started the Drivetime show. We got on really well and bickered like an old married couple on air, but there's only so long he could carry on arsing around and doing the annual Wimbledon Men's Semis joke.

On Christmas Eve 2009 Chappers announced he was going to the toilet and never came back, a reference to our theory about how the Sugababes kept losing members. While some people think he is actually still locked in the Radio 1 loo, I'm pleased to say you can hear Chappers doing proper sport most days on BBC Radio 5 Live.

# THINGS I HAVE LEARNED

## #14: *The* Russell Brand Show *controversy was good for our show*

Back in the early days of the Drivetime show we would do a lot of prank calls. These took many different forms:

*The Chemist Game*
> We would call a pharmacy asking for fictional products with embarrassing names, such as BreezyVag and Anal-Ease. We'd see how long they would keep checking if they stocked the products before they realised what was going on.

*The Bookshop Game*
> This time a book store would be called and asked if they stocked a made-up title, like *Sex on the Beach* by Sandy Flaps.

*The Angry Pizza Man*

One of the most famous calls was to a highly abusive man who worked in a local pizza shop.

*The Takeaway Game*

We'd place an order with one restaurant then put them on hold and link them up to another one. We then asked them read back the order so the second restaurant thought the first was placing an order. It all got completely ridiculous and confusing.

*Florist Calls*

A florist would be asked to write something outrageous on the card to be sent with some flowers. No message was ever refused, even the bank robbery and erotic fiction notes.

*Flirt Divert*

If a listener was asked for their phone number by someone they didn't like, they could give them the Flirt Divert number instead. We would listen to these answerphone messages and air some of the funniest ones on the show.

The prank call is as old as time – or, at least, as old as the telephone – and all of these features were hugely popular with our listeners, but in October 2008 something was to happen that would totally change radio.

On Radio 2's *Russell Brand Show*, Russell and Jonathan Ross famously left a message on the actor Andrew Sachs's answerphone, in which Russell claimed that he'd slept with his granddaughter.

What followed was an immense media storm in which, among others, both Russell Brand and the controller of Radio 2 resigned. The fallout was huge. The papers were gunning for the BBC and everything we did was being heavily scrutinised by our bosses as well as by the media. Radio 1 told us to play everything extremely safe and make sure nothing in any way contentious happened on the show.

I was initially angry and there was a feeling that Russell and Jonathan had messed things up for everyone. If someone was going to cause this much trouble, at least let it be for something funnier than 'He fucked your granddaughter.'

But, looking back, I feel quite a lot of good has come from the Sachsgate fallout.

None of the pranks we did were particularly malicious, but the public were clearly the butt of the jokes and, although we had permission to air them, listening to them now, some of them do make me feel uncomfortable. The whole mood changed and made me realise that we could be warmer in what we do.

We had new constraints and I always believe that constraints are good: they make you work harder to come up with better ideas. We needed new ways to be funny and I think the show has improved for it.

A while later prank calls were back on the show, but with a difference. We had realised it was funnier if the butt of the joke was the person actually making the call, especially if this was Beccy. She was really bad at trying to trick anyone and would soon start laughing at her own incompetence. Beccy, the world's worst prankster, led to the creation of characters like Timmy Trendy, fashion guru to the stars. Beccy's inability to fool anybody was hilarious; the joke was on us and it was funnier.

Beccy Huxtable had joined the afternoon show as Laura's replacement in 2008. I think it was quite hard for Beccy to start with, because Laura had been there for four years and everyone who listened to the show knew her. Beccy had already been working at Radio 1 and was the perfect person to become assistant producer on the Drivetime show, but it's always tough to take over from someone who is really popular.

Beccy fitted in brilliantly and people liked her immediately. Not only is she a lovely person, but she is so sharp and quick-witted. She has become an essential part of the show, and is never afraid to tell me on air if she thinks I'm being an idiot. Items Beccy appears in are some of the most popular things we do, and she's never scared of trying something new.

Chris, who is also on the show now, only started full-time in April 2012. However, I've known Chris for about four or five years, and he's one of my best friends. I met him when he was working on Surge, the Southampton University radio station. I was doing a gig at the uni and he was DJing before me. He came up and introduced himself, and said to let him know if he could help with anything. I thought he had a certain spark about him.

We talked for ages, and then he ended up DJing with me that night. After that, we stayed in touch and gradually became mates. We didn't see each other that often to start with as he was still studying, but I'd meet up with him when I was back home in Eastleigh.

Chris and I have a really similar sense of humour and I liked his laddishness. His stories about him and his mates always made me laugh, and I thought they would be good on the radio. I didn't know where or when or how I could help, but I knew he would be really good on air and promised I'd always keep a lookout for opportunities for him.

When Chappers left there was suddenly a gap on the show. Having the three voices had worked really well but Chappers was a big character and we didn't want to bring someone in immediately, as they would be simply seen as his replacement. It needed to be the right person. Beccy and I worked as a duo for the next year, but I always had in the back of my mind that I wanted to find a guy to join the team.

It's really hard to find someone that you click with and want to spend so much time with. You're basically locked in a studio together for three hours, so you need to get on. Also, to be part of the team you've got to be able to laugh at yourself as much of what we do is about poking fun at each other. We could have got someone in who knew a lot about radio and had plenty of experience, but if they didn't have the right personality it would have been a non-starter.

In 2010 we had a couple of live on-air phone calls with Chris, where I was asking him about nights out he'd had recently and basically taking the mickey out of him quite a lot. I always say he's like a character on *The Inbetweeners*. All of his mates have got nicknames, and they go out and get drunk and get into some genuinely funny situations, which amuse me but make Chris despair slightly.

Ben Cooper, who was by now controller of Radio 1, heard the conversations and asked me about him. Ben said he thought Chris came across as really funny and likeable, and suggested we got him in to try him out. No promises – just to see how he sounded.

Chris came in to do a pilot off air at the beginning of 2011.

It was odd at first because he hadn't done that kind of radio before and felt a bit out of his depth. That actually turned out to be one of his strengths. He's just a very nice, warm guy and that's how he came across. Nothing was forced. He is a normal lad: he likes football and girls and he's very funny without knowing it – he says things all the time that make me laugh, but he doesn't realise he's doing it. He's just himself, which is so refreshing.

In April 2011 Chris started coming in a couple of days a week and doing bits and pieces. He got better and better, and became increasingly confident, as time went on. He brought a new energy to the show. He's a normal lad from Pinner who is everything I'm not, and so there is a great contrast.

It's mad to think that I met him at a gig while he was a student, and five years later he's a huge part of my show. You have to have a good relationship with people you're on air with because it's so obvious to the listeners if you don't. We were lucky to find Chris, and the job is an absolute dream for him: he loves it so much. I love his enthusiasm. He has become the third member of the on-air team, and it's working very well.

It was either my desire to do something different and challenging or my complete inability to say 'no' that meant I agreed to appear on a television show called *Celebrity Scissorhands* in 2006.

It was part of Children in Need and involved a group of celebs being trained to cut hair and do beauty treatments. Anyone could come along to the salon, which had been set up in BBC Television Centre, and get their hair done by us or have some kind of treatment.

To this day I will never understand why anyone would volunteer to have a colonic irrigation on TV; especially not one administered by someone who doesn't have a clue what they're doing. It's like the TV show *Embarrassing Bodies*; if you're too shy to go to a doctor, why get your knob out on TV instead? That's what my mum always says.

I was the lucky person who'd been given the task of the colonic irrigation. Fortunately for the patient, I didn't have to insert anything – there was a trained therapist for that. My job was to rub the client's stomach and look helpful. The poor guy was lying on the therapy table when disaster struck. The tube snapped. Suddenly the man's faeces started spraying all over the room. Shit was literally flying everywhere. It was all over me, all over the walls. As if that wasn't bad enough, the actress Linda Robson then walked in to get her nails done. She saw me and the carnage of crap and shouted, 'What the fuck have you done?' at the top of her voice. The man must have been mortified; there he was, covered in shit with the woman from *Birds of a Feather* screaming obscenities at us. Thankfully, they never showed that part on TV.

One of the other contestants on *Celebrity Scissorhands* was Steve Strange, who used to be in a band called Visage in the eighties. Steve was addicted to heroin for years and had no money, and he was a massive, if rather odd, character. He reminded me of a Welsh Ozzy Osbourne with his eyeliner, Botox and shaky voice. For some reason, he took a bit of a shine to me.

We became friends because there was something I really liked about him. An odd man, and it's fair to say that Steve has had his ups and downs, but I got the feeling he had a heart of gold. He was quite demanding and incredibly high maintenance, and the production staff had to move him to so many different hotels because he kept getting chucked out for smoking and being a bit ... erratic, let's say.

We exchanged phone numbers during *Celebrity Scissorhands*, and one day, long afterwards, he turned up at Radio 1 demanding to see me. When the receptionist told him I was live on air until seven o'clock he replied, 'I could be dead by then.' To say he was a drama queen wouldn't be doing him justice.

He hung around in reception, waiting for me and acting as

oddly as ever. I agreed to pop out for a quick drink with him once my show had finished.

We were friends, but Steve was the kind of person who could easily take over your life if you let him. It was like being his carer: he wasn't the easiest of people, and wherever he went high drama followed.

He had a woman with him on that day, who he claimed was his personal assistant. Usually the role of a PA is to look after someone, manage their diaries and make sure they get to places on time. I couldn't imagine how anyone could get Steve anywhere on time, and also had no idea why he would need a PA as he didn't appear to do an awful lot.

After we'd finished our drinks Steve popped to the toilet and the PA immediately took me aside for a quiet word. She explained that she wasn't actually his PA. Steve had been living in her house for a while but she couldn't have him to stay any more. Steve had nowhere to go, so she asked if I would take him in. With that, she got up and walked out of the pub. Great, I thought. Now I have to look after him. That was a full-time job, believe me, and I didn't seem to have much choice. Where else was he going to go?

Even though he was clearly quite unstable I felt really sorry for him. I said he could come and stay on my sofa for a few days while he sorted himself out. I had to go to Manchester for work the following day, so I had no choice but to leave him in the capable hands of Fraser. Fraser wasn't entirely sure who he was at first, so he sat Googling Steve Strange while sitting next to him in the lounge.

Not only did Fraser catch him putting a whole egg in the microwave so he could watch it explode, but Steve invited himself along to Fraser's comedy gig – back when he was still trying to launch his career as a stand-up – and hurled drunken comments at him all night. You expect the odd heckle if you're doing live comedy, but not from someone you're very kindly letting share your home.

As I travelled up to Manchester I was getting all of these texts from Fraser saying, 'Why the hell have you left me with the guy? He's crazy. He woke me up at 6 a.m. to ask me to wake him up at 8 a.m. This is not normal behaviour!'

When I got back from Manchester I immediately told Steve he had to leave and he didn't take it brilliantly. I'm not great at standing up to people, so I was really proud of myself for staying strong. I think the threat of him staying for ever was also a factor in my assertiveness. I did feel bad for him, but there's only so much crazy you can take.


A lot of odd things happened while I was living in my Kentish Town flat. One day, completely out of the blue, a gnome appeared on the doorstep. This was long after my drunken shopping-channel buying, so I knew it was nothing to do with me, and Fraser had no idea where it had come from either.

The next day, when I opened the front door there were a couple more gnomes sitting there, and a few days later we had a whole family of them. Within weeks there were hundreds of them; our flat was like a gnome grotto. It did freak me out a bit because they were quite sinister in a way; they were all plain white, rather than the cute coloured ones you see in gardens.

I made the mistake of mentioning the mystery gnomes on air. I was made to go and see the BBC police investigator because they were worried it could be some kind of weird stalker. I've never heard of anyone else being stalked by gnomes, so I guess at least it was inventive. I would love to know who delivered them.

I also got burgled. I was on my way home after a first date, with someone I ended up going out with for two years, and the guy in question was going to come in for a drink as he only lived round the corner. As we walked up to the flat I saw some blokes walking off down the road carrying the projector I had at the time. As soon as they saw us they ran to their car, but they did manage to make off with a lot of my stuff. Luckily I got their number plate as they drove off. The police tracked them down and they were arrested soon afterwards.

My new man was extremely supportive, as I was quite shaken up by it. I'd never experienced a burglary before, and they had been through everything. Every drawer had been opened and emptied out. If we hadn't turned up then, they would have ransacked the whole house.

Fraser and I had to go down to the police station and give them a list of everything that had been stolen. Fraser had had some rather personal photographs of an ex-girlfriend nicked, but he'd planned to keep quiet about them.

The police did tell us to declare everything that had gone, so I thought it best to mention Fraser's missing pictures. The police officer got really excited and said, 'That's brilliant, because the pictures will be uniquely identifiable, unlike a TV or stereo, so we'll know for sure if they're yours.'

She asked if I was in the pictures and I replied, 'No, no, but Fraser will tell you all about them.'

I'll never forget Fraser having to sit there, describing the pictures of his ex. I was laughing to the point I couldn't stop, while poor Fraser was bright red and stumbling over his words. The policewoman did her best to keep a straight face.

When the case came to court a list of everything that had been taken was read out to the jury – 'laptop, television … photograph of a woman with … ' You can guess the rest.

# CHAPTER 7

## Sign My Boobs

## THINGS I HAVE LEARNED

### #15: *Lady Gaga is a woman*

Since Lady Gaga first appeared there have been various rumours about whether she is, in fact, a fella. I can lay those theories to rest right here and now.

In 2010 I was doing my usual backstage interviews at the Brits. We had a giant game of Jenga set up in our studio and all of the pop stars who came in had to take a piece out of the Jenga tower, to see how long it would take to fall to the ground. I was chatting to Lady Gaga, and asked if she fancied having a go. She said, 'I don't want to. But I'll kick it over if you want.' Then, the next thing I knew, a Gaga leg emerged from underneath her tiny dress – which was more like a swimming costume – and she booted the Jenga tower. There were giant pieces of wood flying everywhere; I wrapped up the interview and she left the studio. Beccy was filming the interview and had also captured the Jenga moment. As Gaga left I saw a look of absolute horror on Beccy's face, from behind the small camera she was holding.

She whispered, 'Oh my God, I just saw it.' I wasn't quite sure what she meant, but as we watched the footage back while editing it, it was clear that we had seen *all* of Lady Gaga. As she stretched her leg out to kick over the tower, we freeze-framed the video to make sure. Yep, there it was.

I'd not seen many of these before – not close up – but I'd lived with Fraser long enough to recognise this as being a lady's place, a hoo-ha, a gaga, a foof, a gravy boat . . . whatever you want to call it, she's got one and I've seen it.

# THINGS I HAVE LEARNED

## #16: *Never make Katy Perry cry*

Katy Perry is someone who has always been brilliant fun whenever she has come on the show. In September 2010 she said she was up for doing something quite different and we sent her management some ideas we'd written on napkins the night before. After turning down the opportunity to come camping with us, Katy agreed to do an item called You Control Katy (or U CTRL KATY for short).

The idea was that our listeners would get in touch and tell us what they'd like Katy Perry to do, and then she would do it. We streamed this live on the Radio 1 website so everyone could watch as she carried out our listeners' demands in a small TV studio. All was going well as Katy sang, danced, beat-boxed, proposed marriage, recreated the pottery-wheel scene from *Ghost* ... all the usual things you'd expect were suggested.

For a bit of fun we had decided to hire a Russell Brand lookalike. We found someone who was billed as Leicester's number-one Russell Brand impersonator, and presumed he'd be dreadful, which would add to the comedy. When he turned up, though, he did look exactly like Katy's then husband, who was in Los Angeles at the time. It still makes me shudder to think about the moment he walked onto the set, where Katy was spray-painting the back wall. As hundreds of thousands of internet viewers watched, our Russell Brand impersonator wandered up behind Katy Perry and said, in a perfect imitation, 'Hello darlin'!' At that moment everything seemed to go into slow motion. Katy turned round, her eyes taking in who she thought for a split-second was her husband, then came the realisation that this was perhaps a man from Leicester who just looked like him, and she screamed. She properly screamed. And then ran out of the room.

I must have been in shock for a couple of seconds, before remembering we were still broadcasting live. I could see Emlyn's face off camera, and it told me everything I needed to know: Katy was in tears and she might not be coming back.

I stood there with Leicester's premier Russell Brand imper-sonator, and we just looked at each other. Then I remembered the first rule of TV presenting: if the guest runs off in tears and might not come back, wave your arms around enthu-siastically and pretend everything is fine. So I did that for a while, and carried on asking for suggestions from the audi-ence as to what Katy could do next.

In the end 'Russell' was ushered out through the fire exit and we managed to coax Katy back into the studio, but not before she'd put me in my place. She calmly but firmly said, 'How could you do that to me? How would you feel if your other half was on the other side of the world and you were missing him and then someone turns up pretending to be him?'

I could see her point. We'd made a bad call and felt terrible about it, but luckily she carried on being controlled by Radio 1 listeners until the end of the show. Her parting words to me that day were, 'You had better play my fucking records for ever now!' She smiled and winked as she left, but I know she really meant it.

## THINGS I HAVE LEARNED

### #17: *Pick your feuds carefully*

Showbusiness is littered with tales of feuds: Robbie and Gary; Lily Allen and Cheryl Cole; Scott Mills and Katie Melua. That last one wasn't as widely reported as the others, but for a week or so in 2006 it was just as intense. Just like the Katy Perry incident, it all stemmed from a joke that went wrong. We were doing the radio show backstage at the Brit Awards and decided to start a running joke with all the stars we interviewed. At the end of every chat we asked the pop star the same question. It went like this:

> Me: Finally, have you heard what Katie Melua's been saying about you?
> Westlife: No?
> Me: 'Over-rated.'

The repetition of the same joke, coupled with the fact that everyone knows Katie Melua would never be so horrible, meant nobody would take it seriously, surely. As Westlife got defensive and started laying into Melua I realised things were going to get ugly. The head of the Brits stormed in and started ranting at us, Katie's people were livid and what had started out as a stupid joke had actually turned into a feud. Andy Parfitt, the controller of Radio 1 at the time, has never really forgiven me as he had to take Katie's manager and head Womble, Mike Batt, for coffee to placate him.

In a weird twist, when I won a Sony Radio Award in 2010 it was Melua who was presenting the prize. She didn't do it very enthusiastically, I seem to recall.

The first rule of having a celebrity feud is to make sure that both parties know about it. For quite a while I was having a huge feud with Will Young, although he was completely unaware it was happening. In 2005 I did my radio show at a school in my home town of Eastleigh, and Will was a special guest. To be honest, for whatever reason, Will was a bit of a knob that day, and I made the mistake of saying this to a magazine. Before I knew it there was the headline 'WILL YOUNG IS A KNOB'. For years I thought Will and I were enemies; I thought he must hate me, so made sure to avoid him if we were ever in the same place. Then a couple of years ago he guest-edited *Attitude* magazine and I was one of the people he chose to interview. Knobgate was never mentioned, he was utterly charming, and we've got on great ever since.

I think he was completely oblivious to our feud, but on that day back in 2005 it is fair to say he was a knob.

# THINGS I HAVE LEARNED

## #18: *Kylie never forgets*

In 2004 I hosted the *Top of the Pops*/Radio 1 Christmas Party at the Shepherd's Bush Empire with all the other Radio 1 DJs. Kylie was on the bill, and as she's such a big star she was on right near the end. When I went on to introduce her everyone went mental. It was Kylie! I'd bought her songs as a kid, and here I was introducing her on stage. I'd drunk at least a bottle of wine at that point and I got really into the spirit of things by starting to chant 'Kylie! Kylie! Kylie!' The entire crowd joined in, and it was going great. The problem was that it just went on a bit too long. I was on stage shouting 'Kylie! Kylie! Kylie!', the audience were shouting 'Kylie! Kylie! Kylie!', and then out of the corner of my eye I caught sight of the actual Kylie! Kylie! Kylie! waiting at the side of the stage. And it seemed she'd been waiting for quite a while.

Kylie looked at me with that unmistakable 'for fuck's sake, get off the stage' look of hers, but I couldn't stop. You know when you can't judge a situation because you're too drunk? This was one of those times. The chanting went on for about five minutes until I eventually stumbled off and she came on to massive applause. Seven years later, when Kylie came on Drivetime, we had a photo taken together. She put her arm around me and said, 'At least you're not pissed this time, eh?'

## THINGS I HAVE LEARNED

### #19: *Never tell an audience to stop booing Steve Brookstein*

At that same Christmas Party, a lot further down the bill, was that year's X *Factor* winner, Steve Brookstein. He had only won the show a couple of days earlier, and there definitely weren't any of his fans in the audience at the Shepherd's Bush Empire. The show was being recorded for TV so we had to try to make it look as slick as possible, but as soon as I introduced Steve loads of people started heckling. I asked them numerous times to give him another chance, but they carried on shouting.

Finally it calmed down a bit, but the minute he came on and started singing it all kicked off again. I think I was probably partly to blame. I've learned that if you ask a large crowd not to do something, chances are they will do it to spite you!

I remember DJing at a student night where the Cheeky Girls were also performing. They also made that fatal error. When a plastic bottle found its way onto the stage, Monica Cheeky politely asked the audience, 'Please can you not throw bottles at the stage?' You can guess what happened next.

A lot of my spare time is spent DJing at student and club gigs. I am fully aware I'm not a club DJ. I can't mix and I've never made any bones about that; I'm just there to create a party. The sequence of events for these nights is roughly the same wherever I go:

1. Turn up at the venue to find posters advertising the night all over the place. The posters will always feature a large photo of me, taken from the first page of Google Images results. That means the picture is either: a publicity shot from 2004; me sweating in an orange vest after a charity run; a topless me failing the *Men's Health* Six Pack Challenge; a picture of a Radio 1 listener in Mallorca who looks like he's being urinated on; or a photo of Greg James.
2. Get out of the car, look at the posters and mutter something along the lines of 'Oh, for fuck's sake' under my breath.
3. Have a glass of wine.

4. Play some music.

5. Jump around.

6. Have my picture taken.

7. Be asked to sign someone's boobs.

8. Reassure girl whose boobs I'm signing's boyfriend that I'm no threat.

9. Rip poster of Greg James from the wall.

10. Go home.

I've been asked to sign almost everything during my time on the student circuit, from body parts to driving licences and passports. What I've never understood is why people always want me to sign a bit of their body with permanent marker. There must be students walking around for weeks afterwards with my signature on their forehead or left butt cheek. I always explain it's not going to come off very easily, but they're usually drunk so they don't care. I can sign hundreds of autographs a night, so there must be whole universities who wake up with my scrawl somewhere on their body.

I'm honestly not sure if there's a university or club in the country I haven't been to now, but when I first started doing gigs they were generally low-budget affairs. My friend Neil Sloan – who works with me at Radio 1 – and I would drive to wherever the gig was in my old BMW to save money on trains. We'd do the gig, go back to our hotel, have some drinks and then drive back the next day. There was a time when I was constantly being asked to play at a club called Bakoo in Inverness, so Neil and I would have to fly up. We did a lot of nights sponsored by Durex back then, which led to one of the most embarrassing moments of my life.

Neil and I could never be bothered to put our bags into the hold and wait for them at the other end, so we'd shove everything into one bag and take it between us as hand luggage. We'd have two days' worth of clothes, some CDs and loads of condoms to throw out to the crowd.

Once I was taking the bag through security and the bag-scanning machine started beeping, so the bag was taken to one side to be searched. I had no idea what had set the alarm off, but when the officer opened the bag all he could see was a mountain of condoms and a sea of lube.

He started searching through the bag and couldn't find anything that would have set the machine off, so he started taking everything out bit by bit. Including all the condoms.

I was furiously trying to explain that I was a DJ on a safe-sex tour but I don't think he was buying it. Then he pulled out a pair of pink fluffy handcuffs. I honestly had no idea where they had come from. We always ended up with all sorts of stuff in our bag after gigs, from comedy glasses to afro wigs, so they must have been thrown on stage during one of our sets and we'd drunkenly picked them up. People in the queue were laughing hysterically at me as I furiously tried to shove all the sex paraphernalia back in, and I was dying inside. Neil was so bloody happy he hadn't taken our bag through that day.

He decided to christen that group of gigs the Scott Mills Sex Tour 2002, which basically made me sound like I was trying to have sex with as many students as possible. This wasn't the case. I may have woken up in strange places a couple of times but I certainly wasn't taking advantage of the offers I was getting. I got propositioned by girls at universities more than anywhere else, and the offers weren't exactly tame. (If your daughter is currently at university, you may want to skip to the next chapter.)

Long before Fraser was going out with his girlfriend Kirsty he would come along to loads of gigs with me, thinking he might get lucky. He used to get so wound up because really hot girls would offer me threesomes, and obviously I didn't take them up on it. Fraser thought it was a complete waste and used to rant to me, 'This isn't fair. You're gay and they're offering you a threesome and they're really hot. I'm straight and I'm getting nothing.' He got increasingly angry about it, to the point where he stopped coming to the gigs with me because it pissed him off so much.

When girls are really full on I become a bit like a Hugh Grant character. I don't know what to do. I get shy and embarrassed and go bright red, because some girls are so blatant.

I was in Northern Ireland recently and this girl marched up and said, 'I want you to fuck me.' I didn't even know her name! There was another girl who bit my arm to get my attention. I felt her teeth sink into my arm, and searing pain as I tried to shake her off. She was so vicious she made it bleed, and I had to get it checked out by a doctor. A closer inspection revealed a bite mark like you would find in a piece of chicken. She was clearly off her face, as was the girl a little while back who threw up all over the stage seconds after telling me she 'wanted a fuck'.

The front row at gigs can be quite feral. There is a lot of arse-grabbing and hair-pulling if I go too near the front of the stage, and there is always a drunk girl who just stands there, staring at me. At a recent gig one girl filmed me for ages and ages. She didn't talk to me once, even when I asked if she was all right. She kept handing me her phone and showing me that she had written out a text saying 'I love you'. She did that for about an hour on and off, with her handing me the phone, then me handing it back. The message said exactly the same thing every time she gave the phone to me.

Despite all this weirdness, I love doing student gigs. As well as the free wine, posters of Greg James and offers of sex with girls, I also get to talk to people about what they think of the radio shows, and there's usually a plentiful supply of napkins for any important feedback. It's also, let's be honest, a good source of income; a couple of gigs at the weekend and your big food shop is pretty much paid for. There was a rumour in the early 2000s that Dave Pearce had a whole team of clones touring the country, doing tens of appearances each night, and cleaning up. Then it all got messy and now even Dave's own friends and family don't know which is the real him; I heard three different ones turned up for Christmas lunch last year. (For legal reasons I must point out that this may not be true.)

The only grief I get at these events is when guys are there with their girlfriends or a girl they are trying to impress, as if I am a threat! There's been many a time I've seen groups of lads giving me the 'wanker' sign, but I just think, That's fine, you're paying me for this. Carry on.


Although I've visited many universities in the last few years, I have never actually been to one for educational purposes. As I had been working since I was sixteen, I missed out on my own student life, so I can only thank Southampton Solent University for giving me a degree anyway. I'm not entirely sure why, but I was made an honorary Doctor of Arts in 2009. I initially wondered if this was in recognition of my tireless efforts travelling to and from the educational institutions of this country signing boobs, but that turned out not to be the case. I was truly humbled as well as surprised to receive the honour, and on the day I went to receive it my whole family came along. I presume a few of the people who'd actually worked hard for their degrees weren't that impressed, especially when they heard me floundering through the speech I gave.

It's ridiculous: I can broadcast to millions of people or go and DJ in front of massive crowds at clubs, but as soon as I have to get up in front of an audience and speak I crumble.

I used to have this chat a lot with Jo Whiley because she's the same – being on stage absolutely terrifies her. If I'm doing a gig I can have a couple of drinks and be fine, but having to be really serious and talk to a totally silent audience is my worst nightmare. But I got through my speech, and am now a fully qualified doctor. I think.

# CHAPTER 8

# Moving in with The ~~Hoff~~ and Robbie

Being a Radio 1 DJ, a lot of people presume you must have celebrity friends, especially car insurance companies. Their reasoning behind charging me such a high premium is always explained like this: 'Well, you might have Rod Stewart in the car and if you crash he could sue for millions.' It's always Rod Stewart they give as their example; I've spoken to loads of people in the entertainment industry and they're all told they're a high risk because they might be driving Rod Stewart! Never anyone else, it's always Rod Stewart. Presumably Rod is notorious for cadging lifts off of really bad drivers. Or perhaps his backseat renditions of 'Sailing' cause them regularly to wrap their car around the nearest lamppost. Whatever the reason, I'd like to state for the record – and for any insurance companies reading this – that I've never even met Rod Stewart and I hereby promise never to give him a lift, even if he begs. However, the famous people I may actually be driving in my car are potentially even more likely to cause me to crash.

Where Jo Whiley can count Chris Martin and Bono as mates, and Nick Grimshaw is close with the likes of Lily Allen and Florence off of The Machine, I seem to attract a different kind of famous friend, and by different I obviously mean weird.

I first met David Hasselhoff in 2006. I was hosting the red-carpet interviews at the premiere of the Adam Sandler film *Click* in Leicester Square. All of a sudden I heard an unmistakable voice booming, 'I wanna meet Scott Mills. Where is he?' I turned around and there he was, like a beaming, tanned Adonis who'd opened a couple too many buttons on his shirt. He approached and hugged me for slightly too long to be comfortable.

There was a reason for this public display of affection. Earlier that year David had released 'Jump In My Car', a song in which The Hoff attempts to lure a young girl into his vehicle but thankfully changes his mind when he finds out how far away she lives. A campaign started to give David his first ever UK hit, and what better song to do that with than this comical tale of aborted abduction? I urged my listeners to buy the song and give the man what he'd craved for so long: musical recognition in Britain. And they did.

'You gave me my first number one over here,' he enthused, despite the fact the song peaked at number three. 'You gotta give me a call some time.'

I didn't think any more of it, first because I'd feel a bit weird calling David Hasselhoff out of the blue, and second because he'd neglected to give me his phone number. However, when he came to visit my radio show a couple of months later we swapped numbers and he again insisted that I get in touch if I was ever in LA. People often say things like that and you are never sure if they are being genuine, but I was about to go there on holiday so I thought, What the hell, I'm going to ring The Hoff. I had nothing to lose, and it could potentially be hilarious.

I left a message on his answerphone and he called me back the following day – while I was on a coach tour of the Hollywood stars' homes. David told me he was celebrating his birthday in a jazz club that night and invited me along. I was with my best mates, Fraser and Neil, and we arrived to find him having dinner with some friends. We joined them and started making random small talk, although David was clearly distracted. I could see he was regularly looking at a girl on the next table. What followed next was pure Hoff. He smiled at her, then called the waiter over and asked him to re-plate some of the food he'd ordered and send it over to her as a romantic gesture. I'd seen something similar in various films, but I think it usually involved a glass of wine or a cocktail rather than the actor's leftover steak and chips.

David announced that he wanted to go on to some clubs so, leaving the object of his affection behind with an unwanted extra dinner, we all got into his massive jeep and set off. We were sitting in the back while he drove, and soon he turned round and said, 'Seeing as we're on Hollywood Boulevard, how about we go and see my star on the Walk of Fame? You want to do that?' Of course we did! After unconvincingly pretending he didn't know exactly where it was, we gathered to look at this brass monument to his career. Say what you like about him, the man has a star on the Hollywood Walk of Fame. The man was once the most-watched TV star in the world. The man voluntarily donates food to attractive ladies in restaurants. And I was on a night out with him.

Next stop was a club called Les Deux, which had row upon row of incredibly expensive cars sitting outside. This was like something from *Entourage* or *The Hills*. The Hoff was introducing me to everyone he knew, and that was pretty much everyone in the place; drinks were appearing from nowhere and all I could do was look at Neil and Fraser and exchange that look of 'What the actual fuck?'

At the end of the night David drove us back to our hotel.

He couldn't have been kinder to us that evening and, although we were weary, he still wound down his window to greet girls and make their day with kind words like, 'Hey, it's The Hoff! Jump in my car!' That night I found out that David Hasselhoff is everything you imagine him to be and want him to be: he is a genuinely nice guy and I've become hugely fond of him over the last few years.

We really got to know each other when a production company approached me and asked if I would take part in a TV show in which I went over to live with David for a week in LA. I never thought he would agree to it but six months later, in January 2009, I was on a flight to America to film *The Hoff: When Scott Came to Stay*.

To this day, when I tell people I went to live with David Hasselhoff it gets the same response. 'You did what?!' I just wish that I had been more awake to truly take in what was happening.

The day I arrived in LA I was ridiculously jetlagged and all I wanted to do was catch up on sleep. I'd arrived back in England the day before, having spent New Year in Japan, and I was utterly exhausted. I'm terrible with jetlag and it takes me days to get over it, which is strange considering the erratic hours I used to work.

This was one of those fly-on-the-wall shows where I had cameras filming me from the moment I got off the plane. In the opening scenes of the first show you see me driving around Beverly Hills, trying to find his house with no clue as to where I'm meant to be going, and it was all for real. I barely even knew my name, let alone my way around LA. I was so shattered I'm not even sure I should have been driving.

When I think back to it I can't really piece that day together in my head. Every time the cameras stopped filming I zoned out and then switched back on when they started again. I will never, ever forget that first day in LA. It was like the weirdest dream you could ever have.

I eventually found The Hoff's house in Bel Air. He opened the door and was exactly as I remembered him, the beaming, tanned, hairy-chested Adonis, while I probably looked like an extra from *Shaun of the Dead* who had just been hit in the face with a shovel.

Having welcomed me in, he said, 'You've got an hour to put all of your stuff away then we're going jet-skiing.' By sheer coincidence, jet-skiing was right at the top of the list of things I really didn't want to do that day. In fact, jet-skiing was near the top of the list of things I never wanted to do in my life. I was terrified of the things.

But I was here to live with The Hoff and live like The Hoff

so, despite my fear and catatonic state, we headed to Redondo Beach, where they filmed a lot of *Baywatch*.

As I clung to the back of David Hasselhoff's jet-ski, screaming and pleading for him to slow down, I wondered if this would be a good way to die. If I was to go, it might as well be at the hands of a man who had once had over a billion viewers of his TV show, on the former location of that show, doing some kind of extreme sport. Then as I opened my eyes and caught sight of a camera crew on a boat, grinning wildly with their thumbs up, mouthing what looked like 'This is brilliant!', I realised that my death would be captured on film for the world to see, and it would have looked like I had been crying. As The Hoff gave the performance of his life, darting through the waves, I begged him to let me get off. Finally he agreed, and I watched from safety as he carried on showing off for the cameras, bombing through the water until he finally crashed, hitting the water hard and badly winding himself.

A break for lunch was called. The adrenalin rush of my near-death experience was fading and I desperately wanted to sleep. David, despite still being quite shaken by his fall, announced that he had a surprise for me. 'Do you like Vegas?' he asked. I hoped he was joking.

The next morning I awoke in a hotel room. I remember staring up at the ceiling, not knowing where I was. I then looked out of the window, saw the desert and it all came back to me. The previous evening had involved meeting up with Jeremy Jackson, who had played David's son Hobie in *Baywatch*. Years of drug problems have left him looking pretty ravaged and I really didn't recognise him. The 'couple of drinks' I'd agreed to turned into a couple more and here I was tired, jetlagged and now with added hangover. It was a perfect mix for another day's filming back in LA.

David was the best host. When the camera crew stopped filming each night and left us together in the house he would show me DVDs of some of his greatest performances, like his Broadway musical version of *Jekyll and Hyde*. Or we'd play a PlayStation game he featured in. Or he'd show me his social networking site HoffSpace. I was slightly concerned when he showed me an entire room dedicated to VHS tapes of *Knight Rider* and *Baywatch*; as much as I love those shows, I was very relieved he didn't suggest we work our way through them.

I've never known anyone to get as much attention as David does, and yet he's truly lovely to absolutely everyone. When it was time to go home I found that I was really sad to be leaving. Although the whole thing was exhausting, and in some parts terrifying, it had been one of the best experiences of my life.

The show proved really popular, so the TV channel decided to make a follow-up where The Hoff came over to London to live with me. Well, that was the original idea, but, considering he's been known to move hotels because the doors aren't big enough, I didn't think my small house in North London would really accommodate him. For a lot of the show we travelled around Britain in a big Winnebago with David's two daughters, Taylor Ann and Hayley.

Being in LA with David Hasselhoff is one thing, but going to your local Chinese with him and your dad is another experience entirely. My dad talking intently about dim sum to The Hoff is something I never imagined I'd see.

Funnily enough, it's my mum who really gets on well with The Hoff. I took David to meet her in Southampton and, despite him getting caught short and needing to wee in her garden hedge, they really hit it off. So much so that he invited her to *Britain's Got Talent* when he had just joined the judging panel in 2010. We were in David's dressing room and he went off to the adjoining bathroom to get changed for the show, but he left the door open so we could carry on talking. We were chatting away, but when I looked up I realised we had a very graphic view of The Hoff naked. There was a massive mirror outside the bathroom that was reflecting him and his bits into the room in all their glory. Suddenly he realised and quickly closed the door, but all I could think was: my mum doesn't need to see that! But she did.

It's weird with The Hoff now because I feel I've kind of become like a part of his family. The nice thing is that he totally trusts me. He's been stitched up by quite a lot of people in the past – selling stories and all sorts – so he can be wary of new people. I just think he's so nice people sometimes take advantage because they can. He's almost too naive to be a celebrity.

## THINGS I HAVE LEARNED

### #20: *Always accept an invitation from a pop star to visit their home. It will never be what you expect*

When Robbie Williams released his album, *Reality Killed The Video Star*, I was asked to do an interview with him. These things would normally happen at the world-famous Tube-train-shaking, funky-smelling, underwhelming basement studios of Radio 1. Occasionally interviews take place in hotels if a star is doing a thousand other press meetings that day. Junkets, as they're called, are always ridiculously awkward. You are given a random length of time, such as seven minutes, in a hotel room with the star. Obviously, once you've used the tea and coffee-making facilities and stolen the shortbread there's very little time for anything else.

There is also always a publicist staring at you suspiciously throughout the interview, and publicists never smile. Even if you and the star are rolling around laughing at a witty anecdote they've told seven times already that day, you'll look up to see the face of doom staring back at you. One particularly awkward moment came when waiting in a hotel room to interview a famous singer and actress. While she was freshening up in the bathroom before the interview I was nodding and smiling at the publicist while probably trying to sneak the complementary biscuits into my pocket. Suddenly the face of doom turned into the face of panic as we both realised the walls in this particular hotel were paper thin. The superstar singer and actress was having a wee and we could hear everything. I'm not sure if she had drunk a lot of fluid or if time just seemed to stand still due to the awkwardness, but the noise seemed to be deafening and never-ending. The publicist and I stared wide-eyed at one other, wishing the sound would stop. Just when we thought it was about to finish it seemed to start up again. After what felt like an eternity, she emerged from the bathroom and was greeted with the shocked-looking faces of myself and her publicist, both of us with eyes like saucers and rictus grins plastered to our faces. I can't say who it was, but she's the kind of star you couldn't even imagine having a wee, let alone pissing like a racehorse.

Robbie Williams likes to smoke. At that time, he could not go more than a few minutes without lighting up, so the Radio 1 studios were out of the question for the interview, as was a hotel. Instead I was invited to his home in London. It was actually an apartment he had bought for his mother in Chelsea, but Robbie stays there when he's in town. I have always got on well with Robbie and the interview went very well. As I was leaving he asked for my email address and, like The Hoff's invitation, I didn't think any more about it. But, not long after, I received a message from him. The email was written all in capitals and he was inviting me back to his flat. This wasn't a request for a follow-up interview or even a casual chat. This was an invitation to Quiz Night.

Robbie doesn't go out much; he is teetotal, so going to bars has no interest for him whatsoever. Instead, one of our country's biggest pop stars regularly invites people he knows to come and visit him for evenings of parlour games. This is not an invitation I was going to turn down, and I arrived unfashionably early to discover I was the first person there. Plates of sushi filled the tables and Robbie buzzed around excitedly, tidying up around me. Soon afterwards we were joined by James Corden, the actress Susie Amy and Peter Jones from *Dragon's Den*. It was like the line-up for a TV panel show, except there were no cameras and we were in Robbie Williams's front room. Everyone else seemed to have been to Quiz Night before, so they all knew the protocol. Nothing could get started until the adjudicator arrived. Luckily it wasn't long before the doorbell rang and the adjudicator entered the room. It was Gary Barlow. Looking back, I guess his refereeing of Quiz Night must have given him great experience he could transfer to organising the Queen's Jubilee concert, but at that moment nothing was more important than Quiz Night and the games were about to begin.

I say games but in actual fact there was only one game, Who's in the Bag? The rules are simple: you pull a slip of paper bearing the name of a celebrity out of an orange Sainsbury's bag and your mission is to describe the person, without mentioning their name, so that your team mates can guess their identity. We played this for four hours.

It was probably one of the most star-studded but least glamorous evenings I could imagine, and I loved every minute of it.

When the game finally came to an end the other guests quickly jumped to their feet. They all knew the drill: there is no hanging around after Quiz Night. The bag was put away and Robbie thanked us all for coming, then ushered us out the door.

I think Robbie must have seen something about me that he liked – probably how seriously I took Who's in the Bag? – because soon I was invited to stay with him in Los Angeles. Some people will go on a rock-climbing or windsurfing holidays; I went to LA for a parlour-games vacation. To be fair, it wasn't an entire week of Who's in the Bag?, and Robbie was an incredible host. I didn't want to impose so I had booked into a hotel, but he insisted I stay at his house in a ridiculously celebrity-filled gated community. I had previously been past the place on a homes of the stars bus tour. Now not only was I actually allowed in, I was staying there. The nearby houses belonged to Paris Hilton, Tom Jones and, most interestingly, Charlie Sheen. This was around the time of his very public meltdown, and various ladies would arrive at his house at all times of the day and night. Rumour had it that Charlie would regularly wake to find one of his house guests had left, taking one of his expensive cars with her. One girl drove his new Maybach off a cliff, and he only realised it was missing when the police contacted him to let him know. Another great thing about owning a Toyota with Scott Mills written on the side is that nobody – I repeat nobody – would ever steal it.

The morning after I arrived in LA I woke up early because of the jetlag. Robbie doesn't get up early, and neither would I if I were him, so I decided to hire a car and explore. As I was walking out of the driveway his assistant ran after Ste, my boyfriend at the time, and me and said, 'Don't go and hire a car, borrow one of Robbie's. He'll be so offended if you don't.' I ended up driving around in his Jaguar, utterly terrified of pranging it. Every time I drove that car I felt sick; I crawled at snail's pace along Sunset Boulevard, constantly worried about putting an expensive dent in it. When I returned the car to Robbie for the final time I turned the key to switch off the

Gaga scares me at the Big Weekend in Carlisle.

Rihanna grabs my chops at another Big Weekend, this time in Bangor.

The one and only Wing with me and Kelly Osbourne after an incredible performance at the Big Weekend in Maidstone.

*Let's Dance for Sport Relief*. Me and Murs in our LMFAO outfits.

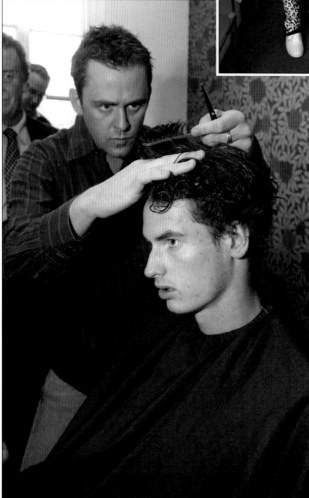

*Celebrity Scissorhands*: snipping at Andy Murray's barnet.

n Kenya on the desert trek. Lorraine and I soak our feet.

he longest, hottest walk ever. Dermot was a great support.

With Frank Mugisha on my first day in Uganda.

The healers who hit me with chickens to cure my gayness.

© BBC Photo Library

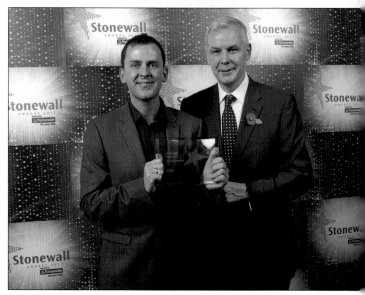

Winning a Stonewall Award for *The World's Worst Place to Be Gay?*

Dr Mills.

The team: me, Chris and Beccy. She does actually have eyes.

A Eurovision cuddle in Baku with Coxy.

Me and The Hump on the way to Azerbaijan. Still clearly full of hope!

Outside my mum's house with The Hoff.

engine and finally relaxed; I had managed to keep his car safe. I had dreaded the awkwardness of apologising for a huge scratch and offering to pay while he told me not to worry and that his insurance would cover it, and that he didn't really mind. Though a few weeks after I arrived home he did email me the three parking fines I had unwittingly run up.

## FREQUENTLY ASKED QUESTIONS

### #4: *What's Chris Moyles like?*

This is one of the questions I'm asked the most and my usual answer is 'He's great'. Sorry about that. I know everyone wants a more interesting answer, like 'He's a monster!' or 'He's a secret kleptomaniac', but neither of those are true. Unless he really is a secret kleptomaniac, in which case we wouldn't know.

Chris and I have always got along really well. Well, there was that time when I first started at Radio 1 when he would mercilessly take the piss out of me, but since then we've become good friends.

We both did the commercial radio circuit at the same time and we've worked our way up in similar ways. I used to listen to him when he was on Signal Radio in Stoke-on-Trent when I was on Key 103 and I've always had huge respect for what he does.

For years the newspapers speculated that I was the heir to the Radio 1 Breakfast Show and was waiting to take his job, and as a result they created a mythical Mills versus Moyles war, which doesn't and never did actually exist.

One morning I got up early to go on holiday and, as I was killing time in the airport, I saw a massive newspaper headline: 'MILLS TO REPLACE MOYLES ON THE BREAKFAST SHOW'.

I figured that, if this were true, I'd have been warned about it. I clearly remember picking up the newspaper and reading it, and the person standing next to me in WHSmith's did a double take when he saw I was learning about myself.

It now looked like I was leaving the country to avoid the confrontation, and to be fair that is exactly the kind of thing I would do, but this sent me into turmoil.

I'm the kind of person who really cares what my friends think of me; I can't bear thinking that I've upset or hurt anyone. This often gets me into trouble as I agree to everything because I don't want anyone to feel bad. Just three examples of times I should have simply said 'no'.

1. 'Scott, are you sober enough to DJ?' (Fraser's sister's wedding).
2. 'Scott, can you just say "Cilla Black's Greatest Hits – out now"?' (voiceover session).

3. 'Scott, the show is very simple: you dress in this silver leotard and Dale Winton shouts "Bring on the wall" – are you up for that?' (my agent, 2008).

I never say no because I don't want anyone to dislike me. Weirdly, I actually find this desperation to be liked by everyone really unappealing in other people, but I can't seem to help it myself. And here I was leaving the country while the papers were claiming that Chris and I had been avoiding each other for weeks and barely spoke to each other any more.

I lay on the beach in Dubai worrying, while journalists phoned me trying to get quotes. I spent most of the time feeling stressed about what was going to be written next.

I didn't hear anything from Chris while I was in Dubai, and I didn't contact him either. I thought it was for the best because I wanted to see him face to face. He knew the score, that I wasn't trying to do anything sneaky and there was no truth in what was being said in the papers.

It really did start a whole feeling that I was trying to take over from Chris, though, so I'm now mightily relieved that that's all come to an end.

I still can't say 'no', however, and recently bought a wagon-wheel coffee table like the one in *When Harry Met Sally* just because the sales assistant was looking disappointed in me.

# CHAPTER 9

## The World's Worst Place to Be Gay

In the summer of 2010 I had a meeting with a guy called
Danny Cohen, who was the controller of BBC3 at that time.
We used to meet every now and again for a catch-up because
I'd done several shows for the channel, and at that particular
meeting he said to me, 'We're doing this programme about
gay rights in Uganda, called *The World's Worst Place to Be
Gay?*, and it doesn't have a presenter attached to it at the
moment. Is it something you would be interested in doing?'

If I'm being totally honest, I didn't know a lot about the
subject at the time so I couldn't give him a definite answer.
Uganda was not really on my radar.

Danny gave me the producer Chris Alcock's phone

number and I called him for a chat. Chris explained that in Uganda some government officials were trying to push through a bill that would make homosexuality illegal. It meant that if you were caught engaging in gay sex they could put you in jail. If you were deemed to be a 'repeat offender' and you 'carry on being gay', you could be imprisoned again, and potentially be sentenced to death. I was absolutely stunned.

I watched loads of YouTube videos to try to find out more. I saw pastors and preachers spreading hate across the country by holding anti-gay meetings. A pastor and activist called Martin Ssempa was the ringleader. He preaches about how being gay is a crime. I found a video of him from 2010 in which he claims to have done research into what gay people get up to in their private lives. He gave the most unbelievable speech in a church about how gay men eat each other's 'poo poo', and declared that Ugandans did not want the 'sickness' of gay people in their country. He showed a really explicit gay porno video and said that it was necessary, so as to educate people about what gay people did to each other. It was extreme, but it would have been just as easy to unearth a fetish video involving a straight couple. He had clearly found the worst possible example he could and he was using it to provoke hatred. But at the same time it was so absurd it almost didn't seem real.

Ssempa whipped up all of this public sentiment because so many people saw the YouTube video and, inexplicably, less educated people believed that was normal gay practice. He also claimed that homosexuals were recruiting schoolchildren, as if being gay was some kind of evil cult. His speeches bolstered the massively homophobic views many in the country already had.

There's another Ugandan man called David Bahati, an MP, whose views on gays are just as strong. As well as wanting life sentences for gay people, he tried to push through an anti-homosexuality bill calling for a new offence of 'aggravated homosexuality' to be brought in. As part of this he wanted gay people to face the death penalty if, for instance, they had sex with someone of the same sex who was disabled or who is under the age of eighteen, or if they were HIV positive. Some of this made sense, of course, because these actions are wrong, but it stirred up even more hate for gay people who were just trying to get on with their lives.

The bill had since been revised so that gay men and women can't legally be killed any more, but that doesn't mean they can't still be locked up for a long jail term.

Bahati believes that homosexuality is a learned behaviour that can simply be unlearned, and that being gay isn't a human right. Not only does he claim that people in Uganda are recruiting children and turning them gay, but he thinks that gay men and women are coming into the country from outside in order to corrupt kids. And I was pretty much accused of this when I travelled there.

There is a very small group of pro-gay activists in Uganda, which is headed up by a man called Frank Mugisha. They were trying – and still are – to battle the bill all the way and make their voices heard. It's a massively brave, and sadly extremely dangerous, thing for them to be doing in such a prejudiced place. Homosexuality is illegal in thirty-seven African countries, so they're a very small minority doing what they can to try to change things.

Once I'd done a lot of research I knew that, even though I was petrified by the thought of it, I wanted to take part in the documentary. I'd never been to Uganda before and I had no idea what to expect. I wanted some reassurance that I would be safe, because once you are there it is hard to judge what is really happening; the same rules don't apply as they do in other countries.

The team assigned to the documentary had been on the front line in Afghanistan and they had also worked under-cover to expose trafficking for various documentaries. Chris assured me we would all be fine. They were highly experienced in tense and volatile situations. I still felt very vulnerable because it was all so new to me. I'd never made a documentary before, let alone one about something so controversial. I think the fact that it was unknown territory was probably what eventually made me agree to the project.

A few days before I was due to go to Uganda all of my friends started asking questions about whether I was doing the right thing and I got cold feet again. I rang up the head of BBC News to ask if we would have security travelling with us, and he explained that while we wouldn't have bodyguards as such, we would have two Ugandan 'fixers' who knew the lie of the land and what to do if there was any trouble. We were going to be a very small team: just me, the producer, director and cameraman, Chris and Janey, the assistant producer, so we needed to work closely and support each other.

I held off from telling my parents exactly why I was going to Uganda. I told them I was making a programme, but I left things very vague because I didn't want to worry them. I certainly didn't mention that I could be in danger. As much as anything, I didn't want to admit that to myself.

Before I left I travelled to Portsmouth to meet a man called John, as part of the programme. He had fled Uganda after being persecuted for being gay. Friends of his were beaten up and tortured until they revealed identities of other gay men, and his name was given. As a result, he was shunned by his family and had to go into hiding until he was able to come to the safety of the UK. He said he lived in constant fear of being beaten or set on fire while he was back home, and if he were to return he would most likely be killed.

As I made my way to the airport I once again questioned why I was going somewhere that was incredibly dangerous for me to be, and I definitely had reservations. But I had committed to it, and so I had to trust that everything would be okay.

Arriving in Kampala, Uganda's capital city, was a massive culture shock. I'd never seen an airport like it before in my life. People were begging everywhere, even as I was getting my suitcase from the carousel, and it immediately became obvious that this was going to be an encounter like no other. The airport was pretty much a shack and when we first walked outside it was unlike any other experience I'd had before. It was so humid, and the road was like a dirt track and incredibly busy.

Our 'fixers', Josh and Steve, met us at the airport in a beaten-up old van and we set off. It was dark but there were no streetlights so you couldn't see where you were going. I honestly didn't even expect to last the journey to the hotel. The potholes in the road were so big you would no doubt be injured if you weren't wearing a seatbelt. Every time we stopped in traffic people were weaving in and out of the cars, and they even did this when the cars were still moving. Horns were screeching and huge trucks kept shooting past us at ridiculous speeds, missing us by inches. I breathed a sigh of relief every time one went past without smashing into us.

The city as a whole was a huge assault on the senses. I've been to Bangkok before, and until I arrived in Uganda that was the craziest place I'd ever visited, but that was nothing compared to Kampala. It was both shocking and fascinating, but I didn't initially feel unsafe.

The security at the hotel was a surprise. When we arrived they first checked under the car for bombs, then we had to go through airport scanners in reception and have our bags searched. It's not a holiday destination by any stretch of the imagination, but a lot of UN workers go out there so the hotel was obviously geared towards them. It was clean, and it had a bar and what could just about pass for a swimming pool.

It was eleven at night when we checked in. I dumped my bag in my room and headed back downstairs. Whenever I arrive somewhere I can never go straight to bed, no matter how tired I am, because I like to investigate a bit.

I got a vodka and Coke from the bar and sat outside on the balcony, which overlooked what was supposed to be a golf course. It was boiling hot, even though it was so late at night. I was mulling over what could possibly lie ahead in the coming week. I was completely in the dark; I had no idea, no matter how hard I thought about it. I called my mum and dad and they asked what Kampala was like. To be honest, at that point, while I was sitting in the hotel, it seemed strangely normal, though it was obvious I was in an African city. I could hear music pumping out of a club near by, where people were singing old Whitney Houston songs on karaoke. It was the calm before the storm.

We were all up at six the next morning to film, and that's when the reality of life in Uganda kicked in. Not just for gay people, but for many of its residents. I have never witnessed such awful poverty; I could have cried at some of the things I saw. It was horrifying and fascinating and sad all at once.

I went across the road to the mini-market because I wanted to have a look at the local newspapers. I had heard that a lot of anti-gay articles are printed, but I didn't expect them to be so extreme. The Ugandan versions of the tabloids have had pictures of gay men on the front page, naming and shaming them. One had the headline 'WE'VE NAMED MORE HOMO-SEXUALS WHO LIVE IN YOUR AREA'. Underneath were rows of photographs of men, along with their name, age, what car they drove and where they lived. They are treated in the same way that paedophiles might be.

Homosexuals are literally hunted down as a result of these newspaper stories. Also, if someone recognises them they are often beaten up or have stones thrown at them. It's a huge witch-hunt, and people are scared even to leave their houses.

As a general rule, Uganda isn't as unsafe as some other

African countries. When I did a desert trek in Kenya for Comic Relief, we stayed in Nairobi beforehand and I was told that I couldn't leave the hotel on my own because there was a large chance I'd get mugged. In Kampala I could walk around quite freely. But obviously it would have been a different story had it been known I was a gay man.

People were really friendly and very welcoming while we were making the programme. They were happy to stop and talk, but when we started asking how they felt about homosexuals we didn't find a single person who thought it was okay to be gay. Not a single one. I spent hours and hours on the streets asking the locals. We wanted to find someone who wasn't prejudiced so we could present a balanced view. But the universal opinion was that it was wrong and homosexuals should be punished. The closest we came to finding someone who wasn't massively extreme was one girl who didn't agree that gays should be killed, but she still thought they should be locked up, away from the rest of society. Ugandan people seem to see prison as some kind of rehab. They think that when you go to prison you learn not to be gay, and by the time you are released you have been 'cured'. If it's discovered that you haven't been cured and you offend again, you go straight back to prison – or worse. It's not unusual for people to go missing after they've been convicted of a homosexual offence.

Despite these extreme views, Kampala can seem fairly normal on the surface. Although it's pretty run down, there are beach bars and restaurants. Ugandans go out and drink and have fun like anyone else. It's just sad that the bitter hatred for gay people is so prevalent; it tarnishes everything around it.

We went to a very cool bar one night, where there were campfires, great music and people dancing. It was a really good atmosphere and I didn't feel at all intimidated. However, we were with some gay activists we'd met who were quite camp, and I did feel like things could potentially kick off if the wrong thing was said or someone decided that they wanted to take a stand against gay men being out in public.

We went to another bar to do more filming, which allowed gays in on Sunday nights. It's all very hush-hush and only people in the know are aware of it. There was a special cordoned-off area for gay men and women to hang out in, and although other drinkers know what's going on, no one says anything. The only reason the owner lets this happen is because he can't get customers in on a Sunday night; it's just to make him some money.

We wanted to do some filming in the bar but as soon as we got our camera out everyone put their hands in front of their faces and started shouting, 'No, no.' Understandably, they were petrified about what might happen if they were identified. Frank Mugisha talked to them, explaining that we were working for the BBC and that the programme would never be shown anywhere in Africa. It took ages for us to gain their trust, and to persuade them that we were not going to stitch them up. They thought that if they were seen on TV it would be the end of them. If you're labelled gay over there, your normal day-to-day life is effectively over.

Once the people in the bar got their heads around what we were doing they agreed to talk to us, but it took some time to convince them. We spoke to several people who had been beaten or disowned, and one poor girl told us she had been raped by a man who wanted to try to 'cure' her of fancying women.

That night really unsettled me and made me want to jump on the first plane home. When I was panicking it was Chris, my brilliant producer, who calmed me down. He's had so much experience with making documentaries that nothing really fazed him. He made me realise that we had to see the thing through. It was strangely exciting in a way.

Of course I expected a high level of homophobia in Uganda, but – perhaps naively – I also expected a large proportion of educated people to think that being gay was acceptable.

We went to visit a group of gay men and women who were

living in the Kampala slums because they were in hiding. It felt tense, and as we walked through to their area we were told not to film at all, so as not to arouse suspicion. They were all sharing one room; they had barely any sheets or blankets and no beds. But to them, it was home, and where they felt safest.

The smell in the slums was horrific, so bad it made me gag. There was faeces all over the street and a river of stagnant waste, which, at one point, I saw a young baby fall into. It was disgusting and upsetting. I was told by one of the locals to listen out for a really shallow cough, as if the person can't get the cough out properly. I heard it constantly and when I asked what caused it I was told it was cholera.

We met with some families and the village elders and, through a translator, we got their opinions on being gay. There was a lot of shaking of heads and angry faces. Their views were clear.

As we were leaving the slums I got my iPhone out of my pocket and a man stood in front of me, stopping me in my tracks. He called me over to his hut and started pointing really enthusiastically at my phone and then at one of his children. It transpired he wanted to swap my iPhone for one of his kids.

*

We really wanted to investigate every aspect of being gay in Uganda, so we went to take a look at Kampala's Mulago Hospital. It was so dirty and disgusting that it looked like the kind of place you would get ill rather than better. There were hardly any beds so sick people were on makeshift beds on the floor. I went to the Aids ward and spoke to this poor guy who looked like he was only days away from dying. Because he had full-blown HIV the hospital had assumed he must be gay and didn't give him the drugs to manage the illness. He has since died, and sadly it was not an isolated case. If you're gay and have Aids, hospitals won't treat you. You have to pay doctors in secret to get the drugs you need to keep you alive.

'Curing' people of being gay is big business in Uganda. It really is believed to be a disease, and as such you can be made 'better'. I went to see a witch doctor who assured me he could make me straight. It was clear from the moment we arrived that he and his friends were taking the piss out of me. Apparently the more money I handed over to them, the more likely I was to be cured. Funny, that.

I asked how long it would take to cure me of being gay, and through the translator I learned that it would be three days. The witch doctor wanted to take me up a mountain to exchange my soul for a cow's. The cow would become gay, and I would be straight. I worried about a gay cow wandering around on its own, shitting itself every time it saw the police. The whole thing was insane.

We explained that as we only had an hour the mountain visit was out of the question, so I was led into a tent and the witch doctor proceeded to chant loudly at me. We then went outside, where he insisted I take my top off while a man waved a giant flaming stick over my head. He then poured freezing water over my head and the witch doctor rubbed me all over with two live chickens. Just your normal Tuesday afternoon. It didn't cure me right away, but I was told to wait a few days and the effects would kick in. I left ten pounds worse off and smelling of ash and poultry. Strangely, over a year down the line I'm still not lusting after Cameron Diaz. What a load of nonsense. I had to laugh as I left, because otherwise I would just have been so angry.

An absolutely amazing man called David Kato featured on the documentary. Along with Frank Mugisha, he was one of Uganda's most prominent gay rights activists but, tragically, in between us making the show and it airing in the UK he was murdered.

Someone went to his house and struck him several times with a hammer in what was believed to be a hate crime. David had recently won a lawsuit against a Ugandan tabloid newspaper called *Rolling Stone*, which had outed him and others by printing names and photographs under the headline '100 KNOWN GAYS (HANG THEM)'.

It was that piece which prompted the BBC to make the documentary in the first place. *Rolling Stone* had run similar stories with headlines like 'MORE HOMOS' FACES EXPOSED' and 'HOMOS WILL RECRUIT 100,000 MORE KIDS BY 2012'. The things they said are chilling. In one piece they even compared gay people to al-Qaeda.

A number of people mentioned were attacked as a result of the articles. Frank appealed to the government to step up security for gay people, but nothing was done. Barack Obama has tried to help but the Ugandan government won't listen. The bigoted attitude is ingrained from childhood.

I find it incredible that people like David and Frank put themselves at such massive risk for what they believe in. Frank is very matter-of-fact about the dangers of living in Uganda, and says that it's just the way his life is.

I desperately wanted to find out why *Rolling Stone* was running such strong, hate-filled stories, so I requested some time with the paper's editor, Giles Muhame. He agreed to the interview, which would be held at Kampala University.

Before the interview began Steve, one of our fixers, showed us where the exits were and told us that if anything kicked off we had to run out as fast as we could, get in the van and drive away. The fact we had a plan in case anything happened made me feel a bit more relaxed. We had no idea how it would go – he could have brought the police along with him or anything.

From the moment I met Giles he was like a smiling assassin. For some reason he turned up with two other men and it all felt quite threatening. The fact he was very well educated and intelligent was alarming, because I couldn't understand how someone who is obviously rational and smart could have such warped views. I confronted him about some of the stories and photos his newspaper had printed, but he had no regrets. He showed no remorse whatsoever, and said he was just exposing wrongdoing. When I told him I was a gay man his lip curled slightly and he said, 'That's what you do in your country, but here it is not allowed.'

I wouldn't say I enjoyed the interview but it was a real eye-opener. I had never met anyone like him before and I never want to again. But in Uganda, that was unavoidable.

I wanted to speak to Martin Ssempa but he flatly refused to do an interview on the grounds that he was sick of being 'misquoted by the West'. I did, however, manage to get some time with David Bahati, the guy responsible for trying to pass the anti-homosexuality bill. At first he refused to talk to us, but we persevered and eventually convinced him that we needed his opinion to make the documentary credible. We wanted to give him the chance to explain his reasons for what he believed in.

He would only be interviewed in the government building in Kampala, which was instantly quite worrying. He kept us waiting for hours, then for some reason we were thrown out of the building and told we would have to interview him in the garden outside. In hindsight, I'm very glad we did do it outside, because it made it easier to get away. If the interview had been held in the building, which was the original plan, I hate to think what would have happened.

We set up the camera on the lawn and Bahati came out smiling. He was initially very friendly. I questioned him about his views and was quite challenging towards him. He spouted all this nonsense about how parents should report their children if they're gay so they can be rehabilitated, and then he said, 'If one gay man can come to me today and say that they're a gay man and it hasn't been taught to them and they were born that way, they must do it.' I knew it was my chance, but I can't deny I was scared, and hesitated for a long time before getting the nod from Chris from behind the camera. Two or three times I had the chance to tell him, but at the last minute I bottled it and asked another question instead. Eventually I came out with it: 'Well, I'm a gay man and I believe that I was born that way.' I knew full well he would never have agreed to speak to me if he had known.

Although I was feeling very shaky I asked him what he was going to do to me. He replied, 'It's a good job the police aren't here. I could arrest you now.' He also recommended I didn't get 'caught in the act'. He then ripped his microphone off and walked away. He was clearly very angry, and was saying he had been hoodwinked by the BBC.

Steve said we had to get out of there immediately. We grabbed everything as quickly as we could, piled into the van and zoomed off. About a minute later Josh, the other fixer, got a call from Bahati demanding to know where we were. We could hear him shouting, 'Where are they? Where are they? Find them now! If you do not find them you will never work again.'

Josh covered for us, saying he had no idea where we were, even though he was in the van with us. It was like being in a film. Bahati basically wanted to track us down and take the tapes away from us because he didn't want them aired, and he wasn't about to give up easily. He was calling Josh constantly, saying he was going to find us at our hotel and bring police along to arrest us. Chris managed to keep us all calm, but there were still all sorts of things going through my head.

There are only a handful of hotels in Kampala so we knew it wouldn't be hard for Bahati and the police to find us. To throw them off the scent Josh told Bahati that he thought we were staying at the Hilton, which we weren't.

Apparently Bahati and the police later turned up at the

Hilton, asking which room we were staying in and saying they were going to arrest us. By this point we were back at our hotel, minutes down the road from the Hilton, and I was feeling quite panicked. We called the head of BBC News to get some advice about what to do and how to stay safe. I was absolutely beside myself with worry. We were advised to stay in one room together to minimise the likelihood of being found. We had to persuade the hotel staff to say we weren't staying there. If anyone asked, they were to say they had no knowledge of us. We weren't due to leave for another two days so we were under house – or rather hotel – arrest.

Could they have arrested us? Who knows; it seemed very possible. We were in their country, with their laws. Josh told us stories about people who had been taken out to the country by the police and beaten, or worse, which didn't help with my nerves. It became clear that Uganda is utterly lawless at times.

We still had the tapes of the interview with us so we gave them to Steve to take home. We knew that if the police found us with them they would take them from us, and we didn't have the power to do anything about it.

Come the evening I went back to my own room, double-locked the door and tried to sleep, but it was impossible. I read for a while, I called some friends from home to try to feel a bit more connected and reassured – you name it. I kept picturing the police guys knocking on the door, and tried to work out what the hell I would do if they did.

David Bahati called up the head of BBC News in London himself and told him that the BBC was not allowed to broadcast the tapes. They had a massive argument, in which Bahati was told that it was in the public interest to air them. The BBC also told him that it was in any case too late to do anything as the tapes had already been couriered out of the country. That wasn't true – they were still at Steve's house – but hopefully Bahati would then give up his search for us.

Steve was due to pick us up at six o'clock the following morning, as usual. We were driving out to a place three hours to the west of Kampala, so at least we felt safer knowing Bahati and the police would have no idea where we were. I'd barely slept and felt really rattled, so I was drinking tons of coffee and smoking a lot.

Steve had always been dead on time, so when it got to half-past six and he still hadn't arrived, we were extremely concerned. Chris kept ringing Steve's mobile but it was going straight to voicemail. It got to eight-thirty and we were imagining all sorts. For all we knew, the police could have followed Steve from our hotel, seized the tapes and done whatever they wanted to him. Even the usually level-headed Chris was pacing around the hotel car park, looking worried.

The waiting was awful. We started to really worry that they had caught Steve. Then, at half-past nine, he finally called to say he'd overslept. He didn't have enough electricity in his house to charge his phone, and he'd only just managed to get it working again. We were so bloody relieved. He was sorry to have alarmed us so much, but we were just glad he was okay. Everyone had grown very close to Steve during the filming, and I went over to give him a massive hug as he pulled up in the van.

We eventually headed out of Kampala, and our first stop was a radio station where we were due to sit in on a debate about homosexuality. Some radio stations had been taken off air for hosting gay debates, so it was a big deal that they were going to be talking about it.

Frank was with us, and I sat alongside him as he tried desperately to put across his pro-gay argument. Listening to the bigoted views of other people on the show was so frustrating that I had to leave the studio at one point. Even the host was hugely prejudiced, when he was meant to be impartial. Once again, it came off as a totally one-sided view.

We all stayed overnight in a local hotel, and my room looked like what can only be described as a cell. I had to wrap myself in a mosquito net and watch and listen as hundreds of mosquitos dive-bombed me all night. All I could hear was the constant buzzing and it was hideous.

Thankfully, we were flying back to London the following day. I couldn't wait to get out of the country. We had drinks with Steve to say goodbye and he told us this story about someone he knew who had gone out for a business dinner.

The only way you can really have money in Uganda is to own livestock and farms. This man was fairly wealthy, and owned a lot of land. Unbelievably, the man he was having dinner with poisoned him so he could take control of the land, and he still owns it to this day. Even though Steve's acquaintance called home from the meal to tell his family that he thought he had been poisoned, there was no way to prove it because there wasn't a proper autopsy – and the man has never been brought to justice. I think that says it all.

We didn't know if Bahati was still after the tapes, so we were a bit wary about arriving at the airport in case he had people waiting for us. To throw them off the scent Janey, the assistant producer, flew back to London via Nairobi, carrying the tapes. Apparently that kind of thing happens quite often when people need to get sensitive material safely out of a country. It all felt a bit James Bond to me, but they said it was necessary. Janey would be the least suspicious because she was the only black member of our crew.

I can honestly say I've never been so happy to leave somewhere. As our plane took off I was like, 'Thank God!'

But what an experience. As much as I was happy to get home and my bed has never felt so good, I was grateful to have been through such an incredible experience. So much happened in the space of a week, it was mind-blowing.

Visiting Uganda made me realise how lucky I am. In London your sexuality, whether you're gay or straight, is not an issue. No one cares, especially in my industry. I think we take for granted just how liberal we are in the UK. Okay, so not everywhere you go is gay-friendly, and there will always be prejudices, but on the whole we are incredibly blessed to have the liberal attitudes we do. I don't have to worry about what will happen to me if I go out, like Frank and his friends, and I hope more than anything that they can stay safe.

I've never had such an incredible reaction to anything as I did to *The World's Worst Place to Be Gay?* Even now I get people stopping me in the street to say what an impact it had on them. I was getting a coffee the other day and the girl behind the counter started chatting to me about it. She said that the programme had opened her eyes to what is often a hidden problem in Africa. I feel so proud to have been a part of it.

The documentary was shown in America, and in November 2011 it won a Stonewall Award for Broadcast of the Year, which was the icing on the cake. To win an award for something that isn't really my skill is fantastic. It was heartbreaking to make and sometimes harrowing, but if I was asked to do it all over again I would.

I went back to Africa less than six months later, this time to Kenya, where I joined various celebrities to trek across the Kaisut Desert in aid of Comic Relief.

It was a pleasure to do something on TV for charity that didn't involve Linda Robson off *Birds of a Feather* swearing at me while I was covered in a complete stranger's faeces.

Compared to the previous Comic Relief expedition where a group of celebrities, including Chris Moyles, climbed Kilimanjaro, walking across a desert didn't sound that hard, so I signed up straight away. How wrong I was. We were warned beforehand that covering a hundred kilometres in five days would be even more physically challenging than Kilimanjaro. When I thought of the desert, like most people I imagined miles and miles of sand, but it was mainly flat land or scrub surrounded by mountains, and incredibly difficult terrain. And it was hot. I was prepared for a desert to be hot, but 48°C? It was without doubt the hardest thing I've ever done.

The aim of the trip was to raise money to provide sight-saving operations and vital eye care for people in Africa. Peter White, from Radio 4, is blind, and it was really inspiring that he was walking with us. I also made some really good friends because when you're walking you have nothing to do but talk and talk. Sometimes there would be complete silence for a couple of hours, and that's when people would pull their hats down over their faces and look at their feet. At that point you knew that everyone was so tired they were ready to collapse. I felt worst for the cameramen and crew, who would regularly pass out because of the heat. On the last day I felt like we would never get there. It just went on and on, for mile after mile.

Dermot O'Leary became the unofficial leader, keeping us organised. Craig David and I bonded over the fact we're both from Southampton. He's exactly as I wanted him to be: funny, smart and keeping himself going by singing his own songs! I've always loved Lorraine Kelly; I couldn't have lasted the five days without her. She now calls herself my TV mum and she looked after me so much. She found the trek really hard going, but something kept her strong. It was Ged, who was like our trek's version of Bear Grylls: an ex-special forces officer who knew about all of the dangers of the venomous snakes and spiders and things. Lorraine loved him. She kept giggling to me, 'He's just so beefy and hunky!' As well as being beefy and hunky and Lorraine Kelly's inspiration, Ged was incredibly reassuring, and kept us going when things were at their worst.

No one had any pretentions on the trip, and to be honest even if they'd tried it would have been pretty much impossible due to the conditions. It's hard to be a diva when you're all using the same hole in the ground as your toilet, and the shower is just a watering can that would slowly tip water over you.

Dermot may be the host of the biggest show on UK television but when it comes to taking a dump in the desert, he's just like everyone else.

The makeshift loo had a windbreaker around it so no one could see you doing your business from the front, but the back was open. One evening Dermot turned around after having done what he needed to do and realised there were around thirty African schoolchildren standing there watching him. He gave them a smile and a wave, and they were completely oblivious to the fact that they had just seen one of our most famous TV presenters having a poo.

There was no such thing as personal space. You had your own tiny tent to sleep in, and as soon as you unzipped it in the morning that was it – you were a team again, with nowhere to hide. We each had a little bowl we'd fill with water and Dermot would be washing his face, Lorraine would be cleaning her teeth and Craig David would be singing 'Fill Me In' really loudly in the next tent. It was like a school trip, but with people off the telly.

It was so hot at night it was hard to sleep, but thankfully Ronni Ancona had some sleeping tablets. I have no idea where they came from. After feeling like I barely closed my eyes on the first night, I slept like a baby for the rest of the trip. I had been starting to get really stressed, because if you couldn't sleep you would be knackered for the next day of intense trekking.

This was physically the hardest thing I've ever done, but it was also life-changing in that it showed what I was capable of when I put my mind to it. We managed to raise over a million pounds, which is the most important thing, and I wouldn't hesitate to do something like that again. I came out of it with some really good new friends, and now know every lyric on Craig David's *Born to Do It* album off by heart.

# CHAPTER 10

# Scott Mills: The Musical

## THINGS I HAVE LEARNED

### #21: Never forget your towel when you go to the bathroom

It's summer 2010 and I'm at the Edinburgh Festival. During August, many residents leave the city to avoid the millions of people drinking, singing and, inevitably, puking on their streets. It also means they can make some serious money letting someone else live in their home while the Festival is on.

For our annual week in Edinburgh we have rented a large house for the whole team to stay in; it's a family home and the family has simply moved out. But they've left it exactly how it was: their clothes are in the drawers, there are photo frames with family pictures in every room, their food is in the fridge and the calendar on the kitchen door details all their movements, from dental appointments to violin lessons. It's almost as if the family went to work and school one day and just never came back. This has been quite disconcerting for a few days, and I've had to remember which is my toothpaste and shampoo in the bathroom and which belongs to them.

We've tried to feel more at home by making up names for the strangers in the photos. We agreed on Malcolm's name first, because he really looks like a Malcolm. Then there's his wife Jean and their lovely children Günther, twelve, and fourteen-year-old Fenella. Günther seems to be very good at music, and there are many photos of him with his violin. I think Jean would like him to be a professional musician, but Malcolm is more practical and would prefer he follows a career in the law, like his grandpa Helmut, whose portrait adorns the wall of the study.

Fenella loves McFly, if the posters in her pink room where Beccy is sleeping are anything to go by. She is also good at a sport and has a trophy; however, the plastic figure on the top of the trophy that usually indicates which sport it was presented for has broken off, so we can only speculate as to what she is a champion of. The general consensus is that it's darts.

It's Friday and the last day of our stay in Edinburgh. I'm getting ready to do our final radio show of the week before heading home to London. I've not packed my case yet, although I haven't really unpacked because Günther's clothes are taking up all the wardrobe and drawer space. I step out of the shower and notice I've left my towel in the bedroom, so I decide to make a run for it across the landing. In a piece of typical bad timing, as soon as I leave the bathroom someone comes running up the stairs and we both freeze as they see me there, starkers and dripping wet. I instinctively cup myself and then realise I don't actually know who this person is. This isn't anyone from Radio 1, but I do recognise her face. Then it dawns on me: it's Fenella!

Fenella screams.

I scream.

Fenella screams louder.

I say, 'Fenella!'

Fenella looks puzzled, as if no one has ever called her this before.

She screams again and runs down the stairs.

I rush into the bedroom and quickly dry myself and get

dressed as photos of Malcolm and Jean look at me disapprovingly from the bedside table.

.I hear a commotion downstairs and hurriedly pack my case. The family have come back early. Although they think that it's us who are late leaving. There has been a miscommunication about times and I can hear Malcolm's voice, which is a lot higher pitched than I'd imagined it to be, complaining about us still being there. Poor Fenella, what must she have thought?

I quickly make my way downstairs where our Live Events assistant is showing Jean the rental agreement and, for some reason, explaining who I am.

The whole family look at me as I slowly edge towards the front door wearing the international facial expression for 'sorry'.

As we're waiting for a taxi outside, the front door opens and young Günther appears. He walks down the path, smiles, hands me a small notebook and asks for an autograph.

At least one of the family doesn't hate us, I think, as I write him a note: 'Dear Günther, thanks for letting me stay in your bed, Scott Mills.'

Günther looks at what I've written and then back at me.

He looks disappointed, and walks back into the house.

\*

My love of the Edinburgh Festival Fringe started in 2009. Before then I really knew very little about it, but it's since become my favourite part of the year.

Emlyn and I were asked by Radio 1 if we thought there was anything we could do at the Festival to bring it to a younger audience. Coverage of the Fringe had been very much something for Radio 4 and *The Culture Show*, rather than Radio 1.

The more we looked at what went on in Edinburgh the more we realised there were so many things a young audience would love, if they only knew about them.

If you haven't experienced the Edinburgh Festival Fringe before, it's a whole month where thousands of shows are put on all over the city in venues ranging from concert halls to someone's kitchen. There's everything from music to comedy, cabaret, theatre, burlesque, and some really, really weird stuff. The streets of the city are packed with entertainers and people handing out flyers, trying to persuade you to see their show. Anyone can put on a show as long as they can afford to hire a space; there's no quality control and the whole festival has an atmosphere and a spirit like no other.

A few evenings were spent scrawling on napkins, trying to work out what we could do to represent Edinburgh on Radio 1. Nothing seemed to be exciting us until someone at the Unofficial Mills website emailed me a flyer they had found on the internet.

The hit new musical!

*Rick Rollin'*

... the story of the British male singer, from Cliff to

Astley

It was a very convincing poster advertising a musical at the Edinburgh Fringe and featured photos of Rick Astley and one of myself that I recognised from the first page of Google Image results and posters in many university unions.

Starring

BBC Radio 1's

Scott Mills

as

Cliff Richard, Rick Astley, Leo Sayer, David Essex, Chris de Burgh ...

... and many more!

I would be playing the parts of all these old blokes and singing their hits from 9 to 15 August at the Pleasance Baby Grand.

Of course, everyone else thought this was hilarious and it was even discussed as to whether we should actually stage this *Rick Rollin'* show. I wouldn't have said no, of course, because I can't!

Thankfully the idea of a Radio 1 DJ singing the hits of Chris de Burgh and Leo Sayer was deemed 'unsuitable for our target audience', but the idea of us putting on our own performance of some kind was exciting everyone on the team.

Rob Lewis, who was my radio show's executive producer at the time, was with us in a meeting in late May 2009 that went almost exactly like this:

Me: So if it's not *Rick Rollin': The Musical*, what can we
  do?
Emlyn: What about *Scott Mills: The Musical*?
Me: A musical about me?
Rob: Do you reckon we could do it?
Me: What the . . . ?
Beccy: LOL
Emlyn: Yeah, why not?
Rob: Great! Scott?
Me: Er . . . yes?
[*Beccy writes the words 'musical LOL' on a napkin*]

That's the great thing about Rob: he's not the kind of boss who sits and negatively goes through all the practicalities; he's someone who gets excited by an idea that could be new and different. He always wants to come up with bigger ideas and challenge the way things have always been done in the past. Rob will fight for a good idea, even if it means a huge amount of hard work and headaches. And *Scott Mills: The Musical* would prove to involve a lot of both.

Despite feeling weird about us writing a play all about me, and the fact that I really hate musicals, we agreed that putting on this show would convey to our listeners what Edinburgh was all about, and that we'd also desperately need them to help us write it.

It was to be an immense joint effort; we had around two months to come up with everything: a plot, a script, a cast, some songs, a venue. And that was before we knew about the hundreds of other things we'd need. A director? Lights, anyone?

We called everyone we knew to help us. Tim Minchin, who had just started writing *Matilda: The Musical*, helped with some song ideas, while Adam Meggido from *The Show-stoppers*, where the cast improvise a new comedy musical every night, taught us about structure, and we sat through countless proper musicals to see what we had to include. Did I mention I really hate musicals?

The story we came up with was based on the real-life drama of me getting wasted at the Brit Awards and going on Radio 1 drunk, except that in the musical I get fired. The rest of the action is me trying to win my job back by various means, including dressing as Susan Boyle for some reason.

I'm not going to give any major spoilers in case you haven't seen it yet; it's still on the Radio 1 website if you want to watch it.

Another problem we encountered (apart from my loathing of musicals) was that I can neither sing nor act. Our ingenious solution was to make sure I neither sang nor acted much. In fact, we cast other people to play the parts of us. Patrick Wilde, our director, tracked down some brilliant actors who were all available and, more importantly, not too picky about the work they did.

For the part of me we decided to do a *How Do You Solve a Problem Like Maria?*-style talent search. Listeners applied for the chance to play me on stage and we eventually narrowed it down to a few finalists. To be honest, we weren't swamped with entries, so the narrowing down didn't actually take very long.

In retrospect, I can't imagine what the musical would have been like if Joe Taylor hadn't been voted the winner by our listeners. Would it have been completely different if the fella with the ukulele had won? We were lucky, we had Joe as our Scott and he could actually sing.

The final piece of casting was for the part of The Narrator. David Hasselhoff was in town and we'd arranged to meet for lunch. When we had finished I told him to come to Radio 1 to say hello to everyone as he'd not been in for a while. As he walked through the door of the studio he encountered a film crew, lights and Beccy holding up huge pieces of paper with our script for him written on it. He was taken aback at first, as you would be, but I quickly explained that we needed him to read a few lines for a video which we would project onto the stage at the theatre. He really didn't understand why but, because he's so lovely, he agreed. I felt slightly guilty about ambushing him, but explaining the concept to him before-hand would have taken days. The only problem was that David didn't have his glasses with him, so if you watch the musical carefully you'll see The Hoff squinting to read his lines every so often.

David was also confused as to why he was playing The Narrator and I was playing the part of him. I quickly explained that Joe Taylor was me, Laurie Hagen was playing Beccy and Beccy was playing Jo Whiley. The look on his face was something special. It's that look that says, 'Spoons?'

For the next couple of months we lived *Scott Mills: The Musical* day and night. Then finally, on 11 August 2009, we played the first of three nights at the Pleasance Theatre in Edinburgh. All the hard work had been building up to this moment. I just wanted people to like it; we were so close to it and had heard the jokes and the songs so many times that we had no idea whether it was actually funny. As the house lights went down there was a cheer from the audience. I just remember seeing the actors' faces: they had never played in front of a Radio 1 audience before; the audience doesn't scream like that at the start of *The Taming of the Shrew*. The actors all had massive grins on their faces as they went out onto the stage. As soon as we were into the performance I knew it was going to be fine. The audience got the jokes and I was really enjoying myself. And I *hate* musicals.

The next day the reviews came in: they'd given us five stars. That's five out of five, by the way, not five out of a hundred. We couldn't believe it; the next two nights flew by and before we knew it our first Edinburgh was over. We vowed to return each year and do something else at the Festival, and we have.

'My Pinot Grigio'
From *Scott Mills: The Musical*
*Words and music by Radio 1 listener Paul Christie*


My days are long, the road I walk, the cross I bear,
It would be so wrong for me to come home to no one
   there.
In an empty house, in an empty street, in an empty
   world where I'd live
If it weren't for you and all you have to give.

My pinot grigio! Staring up at me.

My pinot grigio! How sweet a life can be.

Nothing in the world compares with you –

You're actual class.

I like you in my, love you in my, WANT you in my . . .

  GLASS!

My pinot grigio, my pinot grigio.


# THINGS I HAVE LEARNED

## #22: *If you write a fad diet book, I will buy it*

One of the reasons I liked radio so much was because I was so self-conscious about how I looked. My weight has always been something I've struggled with, but I didn't really care enough to do anything about it until I came to London to work at Heart.

One of the girls who worked there came into my studio one day and I noticed she'd lost a lot of weight really quickly. She explained that she'd been going to a doctor on Harley Street who specialised in weight loss. You would eat fish, meat and eggs for three weeks and lose a stone. This sounded perfect, and dead easy.

I booked myself in for an appointment and was surprised when the Harley Street doctor told me to pull my trousers down. There had been no mention of this earlier. Why did she want me to drop trou? Suddenly there was a sharp pain in my right butt cheek as she injected me with vitamins. As my eyes watered and I pulled up my jeans she gave me some green, white and blue tablets to take when I ate protein. I did lose a couple of stone in around six weeks, but the smell! When you work with other people in a small radio studio, and stay there for four or five hours at a time, the whole room can very quickly start to smell like a teenage boy's bedroom. Now add to the mix a DJ who is constantly eating ham and eggs. People would come in and, before they could complement me on how slim I looked, would almost pass out from the eggy stench.

Over the years I've tried the no-carb diet, the cabbage soup diet, the baby food diet, and even the maple syrup diet that Beyoncé was famously said to have done.

In 2011 I went to a detox boot camp in Turkey with my friend Jemma. While we were there we lived on nothing but juices, thanks to a man called The Juicemaster. It was like being in rehab; we were stuck on the top of a mountain with no shops or restaurants; we were totally cut off. After a while my skin was amazing, my eyes were clear and I felt really good, but I was craving solid food. All everyone did was talk about food. I may have looked great but I'd bore you to tears reminiscing about the last time I had a chimichanga.

These days I'm just eating healthily and doing exercise; I

know deep down it's the best diet there is, but I guess I'm just waiting for the next fad diet book to come along and make it look easy. Let me know if you write one, because I *will* buy it.

I've recently relaxed a lot more about how I look. When I was working on *Top of the Pops* I thought everyone was gorgeous and didn't know how I could compete. I was just young and surrounded by pop stars I would never look like. I was constantly comparing myself to celebrities and wondering why I didn't look like them. That's no good for your self-esteem.

Viewers only ever see pop stars at their absolute best, but the reality can be so different. I've seen so many pop stars turning up for interviews looking hungover and a bit spotty. Two hours later, after a heavy hair and make-up session, they emerge looking amazing. I promise you, without their Glam Squad they look like the rest of us. In fact, Katy Perry without make-up really does look exactly like me. This is true: look up a photo.

# FREQUENTLY ASKED QUESTIONS

### #5: *How much cosmetic surgery have you had?*

Whenever I go on holiday, the other Radio 1 DJs will joke about which procedures I'll be having done this time. Will I be having my left bum cheek lifted? Am I having a nipple implant? Am I opting for a testicle tuck?

This all stems from the time I went abroad and came back with new teeth. It's the only cosmetic work I've had, but people think I'm always off on plastic-surgery safaris, where they wheel me out in bandages to see the giraffes while my scars heal.

I will never regret getting the new teeth. When I was about eight and my adult teeth had just come through, I had a bad fall in the playground and cracked both of my front teeth. The dentist put plastic caps on, but they looked terrible and kept falling off. Without the caps they were a strange V-shape, so I'd never been happy with how they looked.

I was doing a student gig in Lincoln about six years ago and I managed to whack myself in the mouth with a microphone. One of the caps flew off, and I was left with one fang and one normal tooth. They were like that for months and I kept telling myself I had to get them seen to. I was very aware of how awful they looked, and for ages I didn't smile properly, so people couldn't see my Dracula tooth.

I was in Dubai on holiday a short while later and I looked into getting my tooth fixed because at the time it was much cheaper to get them done over there. I went to a cosmetic dentistry surgery and the scary American dentist – who looked and sounded like George Bush – told me very bluntly that I needed eight of my top row of teeth capped because they were a mess. He offered to cut me a deal to get the whole lot done. The cost was the equivalent of having three teeth treated in the UK. I wasn't about to say 'no', as you know I am unable to. Plus, he had his hands in my mouth at the time.

While my friends were at the beach every day, I was at the dentist having all of this work done. He had to file down my teeth and place oversized temporary teeth over them. They were so big I looked like one of the Bee Gees. My friends and I went out for dinner on the first night I had them on, and both of the front teeth got stuck in a bread roll.

I was at the dentist until seven o'clock on the night we were flying back to London. I barely saw the sun the entire time I was in Dubai, so came back paler than I was when I flew out. Nobody seemed to notice my lack of tan, though: they were probably too busy cowering from the brightness coming from my mouth.

I hadn't been warned about a worrying side effect of my new teeth, which really freaked me out for quite a long time. They looked great but every time I spoke I made a loud whistling sound. It was really noticeable. I'd told the dentist I was a radio DJ, but he still didn't mention that all my links would now be accompanied by a high-pitched whistling. I panicked. How was I going to cover this up? People's dogs would be barking at their radios. I thought I might have destroyed my career. I phoned the dentist, only to be told that it was normal and that the whistle would go as I got used to the teeth. Luckily he was right, and the whistle disappeared before I could get the permanent nickname of Whistlin' Scott.

## THINGS I HAVE LEARNED

### #23: *Don't take TV dancing shows too seriously*

As I've mentioned, I have a problem saying 'no' to anyone, so when I was asked to take part in *Let's Dance for Sport Relief* in early 2012, I naturally jumped at the chance.

It's on prime-time Saturday-night TV, millions will be watching, I can't dance and have no rhythm ... where do I sign?

I was paired with Olly Murs, who can dance, so we were a complete mismatch. My only hope was that people would be watching Olly and not notice me.

We were dancing to 'Party Rock Anthem' by LMFAO. I can't even do the running man, but when Olly and I turned up to the first session with Richard the choreographer he tried to get us both to do it. Olly did it perfectly straight away, of course, but I had to be taken to one side and taught. The gulf in dancing talent was huge!

I was in rehearsals for about three to four hours every single day to try to get the routine right. Olly was on tour so

I didn't see him again until the Friday night before the show. I'd been working hard for weeks, and Olly turned up and pretty much nailed it in an hour. He wasn't even worried about the fact he hadn't practised. He was so calm, whereas I was absolutely terrified.

As another distraction from my dancing, I roped in The Hoff to help us out with our performance. The show was on at seven that evening and he eventually turned up at five with absolutely no idea what he was supposed to be doing. I explained that all he had to do was run on to the stage with a box on his head, and he seemed fine with it.

The producers suggested that we have an extra rehearsal with David because they were a bit concerned about things going wrong. Olly and I did our routine, and then The Hoff decided to tap dance on to the stage. He took so long to get to the middle of the stage he missed the point in the song where he was supposed to take the box off his head. We rehearsed it again without the tap dancing, and that time he got to the right place at the right time but he couldn't get the box off his head.

I had to explain to him that there would be no point in having The Hoff as the big surprise reveal if he was not going to get the box off his head in time. It could be anyone under there.

Just to throw another spanner in the works, one of the other contestants, Arabella Weir, was taking everything far too seriously. She was performing to Kylie Minogue's 'Can't Get You Out Of My Head', naturally.

Arabella seemed to have it in her head that the whole thing was a fix and that Olly and I were destined to win.

Earlier in the afternoon we'd had to film a fake elimination. It was just for the camera crew and lighting people to rehearse how it would all work. We were standing there, *X Factor*-style, waiting for the results and the guy pretending to be Steve Jones, who would be presenting the real thing, said, 'And the first people through to the next round are ... Scott Mills and Olly Murs!' All of a sudden Arabella sarcastically pipes up, 'Well, *there's* a surprise!'

This was now worrying Olly. He had agreed to do the show based on the fact that, if I was his dance partner, there was no way in the world we'd get through to the final. He had booked to go to Las Vegas on the date of the final, and would have to cancel his holiday if we actually got through this round. If Arabella was right and the whole thing was fixed he'd lose loads of money and time off!

Luckily for everyone, the right decision was made and Olly and I were not put through to the big final. Although we later learned there were only about fifty votes between us and the act ahead of us; Olly's face was a picture when he found that out.

\*

To return the favour to The Hoff, I agreed to host a show he was doing at the Indigo Club at the O2, called *An Evening With David Hasselhoff*.

David sang, danced and wore leather trousers, and then we did a question-and-answer session with the audience. I watched the first half of the show out front with the audience, then I went backstage to see him in the interval.

While we were talking I saw him putting on a fake moustache, which he explained was for the opening number of the second half. Then he put on a wig he'd imported from Broadway. Next came a jacket with swastikas all over it – it was by now all too apparent that he was dressing up as Hitler. The blood drained from my face as I suggested that dressing as the Führer might not go down that well, but he was adamant that it would be totally fine because he was performing a song from *The Producers*.

'Do the audience know that?' I asked.

He just smiled and said, 'It's a bit late now, baby!'

It was a disaster waiting to happen and, sure enough, he was splashed all over the papers in his Hitler outfit, with the headline 'HEIL HOFFLER'.

# CHAPTER 11

# All Change

My panic attacks have become much more spaced out over the years. I still have them every now and again, but I understand them and I recognise when an attack is coming on, so I can manage it.

I finally feel that I have some control over the attacks, but they have always been there, in the background, throughout every job I've done. Sometimes a year would go by in which I hadn't felt down or anxious, and I'd think I'd finally cracked it, that I was clear of them. But then something would trigger an episode and the dark times would come back.

The last big panic attack I had was several years ago. Fraser went to leave the flat and there was an ambulance parked in the road outside. I'd had a really bad panic attack in a taxi on the way back from work, so I'd called an ambulance and asked it to meet me at home. I was finding it hard to breathe and wasn't sure I'd make the journey.

When the cab pulled up outside my flat I got straight in the ambulance, where I was given oxygen and hooked up to a heart monitor, and then I was taken to hospital. It was my worst episode ever, but thankfully after I was checked over I was discharged and able to go home.

The thing with panic attacks is that they can easily become a vicious circle: you worry about having them, which obviously makes you even more anxious and hence likely to have a panic attack. When you do have one, you can feel like you're going to die, and you have no control over your body. It is extremely frightening.

Many people seem to think that if you suffer from mental-health problems doctors can give you some magic pills and you'll instantly feel better, but it doesn't work like that. Medication just keeps you on a level and makes you more able to cope with things.

I was on tablets for a long time, but for the past two or three years I haven't needed them. But I know the problem is still there, lying dormant: an attack could come on at any time, when I'm not expecting it. When I get hit with a low period I am aware that I just need to try to ride it out. I just simplify my life a bit and try to look after myself. Sometimes

I need to take time away from everything until I feel more able to cope.

Depression and anxiety are not talked about nearly enough. I think it really helps if people are honest, and it's nothing to feel ashamed off. It's just an illness like anything else, and if you need help it is available, so why suffer?

Alcohol-wise, I still drink but I've really calmed things down. I drink much less often, which isn't hard! When I do drink I don't go over the top like I used to. From early 2000 onwards I had been drinking wine like it was water, but now I'm more mindful of how much I'm having.

It also goes hand in hand with my fitness regime, and the fact that I want to hold on to my relationship. I have been seeing a guy called Brad for over a year now, and he is very supportive, kind and loving; I feel happier and more settled than I ever have with him. I am very aware that I am not the easiest person to go out with, and he puts up with a lot.

I got a big wake-up call about drinking in 2009 when I was invited along to a *This Morning* party, which are always big, boozy affairs. I was completely pissed, talking rubbish to Denise Robertson and telling Eamonn Holmes that he is brilliant, which is obviously true but I probably told him twenty-seven times.

Fraser came to pick me up in a taxi. As it drove down Shaftesbury Avenue he saw a tramp lying on the kerb in a total state. Only when Fraser got out, he realised that the tramp was actually me. He hauled me up and put me into the back of the cab, where I proceeded to tweet random messages to Eamonn, telling him how much I loved him.

The sense of shame I felt the next day was beyond compare. As well as damaging my pride, though, this was damaging my health. In 2009 I went for a top-to-toe health assessment. The doctor told me I had really high enzyme levels in my liver, which had been caused by drinking. He said I needed to calm things down because my liver was damaged. Not to an extreme level, and it could thankfully repair itself, but I needed to take urgent action or risk permanent damage. This was my health and it was serious.

After that visit to the doctor I stopped drinking for six months.

In late 2011 I took part in a TV show called *Inside Out: Dry December*. It meant that I had to give up alcohol for a month, over Christmas.

I had my last drink of 2011 on 30 November, and from then on I aimed to be teetotal all the way until 1 January.

I learned an incredible amount from doing that documentary, particularly about the shocking effects of drinking. I met one guy called Matt, who was only twenty-six and had liver failure. He'd been drinking heavily from the age of fifteen and it had totally dominated his life. He needed a liver transplant, and knew that if he didn't get one he would die.

There is only a one in five chance that he will get a new liver because there's a massive shortage. It was incredibly sad to see someone in such a desperate situation. It really does make you think about the damage that alcohol causes. Of course, we know the statistics, but until you're faced with a situation like that the reality doesn't always sink in.

The first few days without drinking were a struggle, but seeing Matt really struck a chord and made me determined to last the month.

In 2011 I ran the Eden Project Half Marathon in aid of the Multiple Sclerosis Society. My mum was diagnosed with MS about five years ago, when she was fifty-four. I really wanted to show my support and raise some money for the charity. I knew so little about the illness when we found out Mum had it, but I read up on it and wanted to raise awareness in any way I could.

My mum has got what's called primary progressive MS, and it was discovered entirely by chance. She had been having trouble with her right leg, and she also kept getting tired and had back pain, so she went to see her doctor.

Mum was then referred to a neurologist and given an MRI

scan. That was when MS was diagnosed. They originally thought she may have a brain tumour, or had suffered a mini-stroke, so when she was told it was MS she was actually relieved. She says it could have been so much worse. She always tries to look on the bright side!

MS blocks the messages from your brain, stopping them getting through to the rest of your body, so your limbs don't move as they should, and Mum's affects the movement down her right-hand side. Some days she walks better than others and she gets very tired, but she's dealing with it incredibly well. She never complains, and although there aren't any drugs she can take to manage it she still does most of the things she's always done. She still works as an administrator for a civil engineering firm, and wants to stay there for as long as she can.

The prognosis is that she will get progressively worse, but research is being done all the time so we don't know what will happen. We all take it as it comes and hope for the best. She has regular physiotherapy, and for Christmas 2011 I gave her an exercise bike. She uses it every day, cycling about two miles, which helps to keep her leg muscles strong and keep the joints moving.

A little while ago, Beccy from my show was talking on air about a weird sensation she had been experiencing. Every time she looked down, her body felt like it was vibrating. She had been to her GP, who told her this wasn't possible. Within minutes, Radio 1 listeners were texting us telling her this could be an early sign of MS. When you're used to texts saying 'Why U So Fit?' or 'This song is so bad my ears are bleeding', it was shocking to see so many people speculating that there might be something seriously wrong with Beccy. Soon she was having trouble walking and getting very tired so I booked her an appointment with my doctor near to Radio 1, who told her it could indeed be MS and she has been going for a number of tests. Over the last few months she has been through a hellish time of pain and uncertainty and it's made me want to do everything I can for the MS Society to raise awareness of this horrible disease. Beccy is feeling better at the moment and it's so nice to have her back at work after a long period away.

# FREQUENTLY ASKED QUESTIONS

## *#6–#15*

Having read this book you probably have a few questions you'd like answers to. I imagine they are the following:

## *Were you and Jo Whiley ever lovers?*

I don't want to comment on that out of respect for Jo and her privacy.

## Why were you on a carousel ride in Azerbaijan with Jedward?

It was Eurovision. They were representing Ireland. I put my support behind Engelbert Humperdinck. He came second-last.

## Was Badly Bleeped TV really banned by Ofcom?

Technically not banned, but they were really f_____ p_____ o__.

## Does Beccy really look like Matt Lucas?

Only in a certain light. Daylight, for example.

## How can I follow you on Twitter?

@scott_mills

## How many Sony Radio Awards have you won?

Two gold ones. Some other silvery and bronze ones too, I think.

## Would you ever go on Dancing on Ice?

You're only asking that because you *know* I went for an audition and couldn't stay upright so I had to hold onto the side of the ice rink. Just *leave* it.

## *What* is *Beccy's forte?*

This was a radio-show feature in 2009, when Beccy was desperate to find something that she is good at. It turns out that Beccy's forte is in fact clay-pigeon shooting, which was actually the first challenge Beccy undertook. The footage was never aired due to her being deemed extremely good – with some training she could have made it to Olympic standard – which ruined the longevity of the feature.

## *Are you gay?*

For fuck's sake!

## *How do I become a radio DJ?*

Go to the start of this book, read it and follow what I did. The parts involving panic attacks, hypochondria, drinking problems, colonic irrigation and cabbage-soup diets are optional.

## THINGS I HAVE LEARNED

### *#24: Change is good*

The eight-year period I did on Drivetime was by far the best I've ever done. It may sound a bit arrogant, but I think we've been consistently good, and that's largely down to Emlyn and the team I've got around me. It's been such a high for me so, needless to say, I was quite shocked when I was told that I would be moving to the afternoon show. I just didn't see it coming.

I found out that I was being switched on the same day my mum was in hospital. I was waiting in a café over the road from the Whittington Hospital while they were running some tests on her, and my agent texted me and said, 'I know it's a bad time but I really need to speak to you.'

Chris North, my agent at Wise Buddah, explained that Radio 1 was having a change-around and the plan was for me to move to the after-lunch slot, and be on air from one until four. I had suspected changes were in the pipeline because I'd heard that the bosses were planning to shift things about, but I honestly didn't expect my show to be moving. I hadn't seen it coming at all.

Chris explained that Radio 1 wanted to give me a new three-year contract, which was great, but still I had that awful punched-in-the-stomach feeling.

I was feeling really emotional, and the first thing I did was call Emlyn. We'd worked together for ten years so I wanted to be the one to tell him the news. I think that, like me, he was a bit annoyed at first. Then he turned around and said, 'Do you know what? I think it's good. It's a new challenge for us and there's loads of scope to try new things.' That instantly made me feel better, and when I thought about it more I realised he had a good point.

I had been doing the Drivetime show for eight years, which is a long time. Actually, maybe it was time to do something new. I was being offered a secure three-year contract and I was still going to be on daytime Radio 1. I don't know many people in the history of Radio 1 who have been given that kind of opportunity.

Greg James is a good mate of mine and brilliant at his job. I think he felt slightly awkward about it at first, but he had no need to. I genuinely wish him the best of luck.

As for what lies ahead? I'm with Radio 1 for the foreseeable future, but of course you always think about what's coming next. When I leave Radio 1, I will of course be sad. I spent most of my twenties and, by the time I leave, all of my thirties there. That is a huge part of my life. It's the greatest radio station in the world to me and I want to leave still saying, 'I fucking love that radio station!' To have been there for as long as I have is incredible. I will definitely cry when it's time to go.

When I look back on my early days, when I couldn't even leave the house, it seems that I was a totally different person then. Along with my family and my forever-loyal friends, radio has been a constant in my life, and I am so incredibly grateful to have been a part of something I love so much for so long.

Radio has got me through some of the hardest times in my life, and also provided me with some of my favourite ones. I love it just as much today as I did when I used to make my mum listen to my bedroom broadcasts. And long may it continue.

# FREQUENTLY ASKED QUESTIONS

## #16: *Who boffed Ke$ha?*

In 2010 Ke$ha came on the show, and someone spread a rumour that she had had a little fumble with a member of staff at Radio 1. I don't know if it was actually true, but we talked about it on air whenever we played her records, and asked the question 'Who boffed Ke$ha?' People would text in, trying to guess who it was, but we never revealed the answer. It's been infuriating people for years, so I think it's about time. The person who boffed Ke$ha was . . . . . . . . . . . . . . . . . .

. . . . . . . . . . . . To be continued.


Love you bye.

# Acknowledgements

I'd like to thank the following people:

Chris Carnegy, Steve Orchard, Keith Pringle and Mark Story for seeing my potential. Mark Goodier and the fantastic team at Wise Buddah: Chris North, Jess Hardy, Angharad Marsh, John Lawley, Tom Anderson and Sam Gregory.

Sara Lee and the team at Hackford Jones.

Also Rob Lewis, Neil Sloan, Laura Sayers, Mark Chapman and everyone who I have worked with at Radio 1 who is not mentioned in this book, for being creative and so much fun.

Lee Moulsdale, Simon Bennett, Nick Carroll and Stuart Britton, who supported me from the very start.

Danny Cohen for giving me the opportunity in Uganda.

Lorna Clarke, Andy Parfitt and Ben Cooper for making my dream job a reality.

And to my loving family, anyone I may have overlooked and all of my loyal and fantastic friends. I may not say it much, but I truly do love you all.